Lost Mines
and
Buried Treasures
of
Oklahoma

W. C. JAMESON

NASHVILLE, TENNESSEE

Goldminds Publishing, LLC.
1050 Glenbrook Way, Suite 480
Hendersonville, TN 37075

Lost Mines and Buried Treasures of Oklahoma

Copyright © W.C. Jameson, April 2013.

ISBN 13: 978-1-930584-45-7

Cover photo copyright © Steven A. Anderson

Author photo copyright © Joe Smith

Printed in the United States of America

Without limiting the rights under the copyright reserved above, no part of this publication may be reproduced, stored in or introduced into a retrieval system, or transmitted, in any form or by any means (electronic, mechanical, photocopying, recording or otherwise), without the prior written permission of both the copyright owner and the above publisher of this book.

www.goldmindspub.com

Other books by W.C. Jameson

Buried Treasures of America Series

Finding Treasure: A Field Guide
Treasure Hunter: Caches, Curses, and Deadly Confrontations
Buried Treasures of the American Southwest
Buried Treasures of Texas
Buried Treasures of the Ozarks
Buried Treasures of the Appalachians
Buried Treasures of California
Buried Treasures of the Rocky Mountain West
Buried Treasures of the Great Plains
Buried Treasures of the South
Buried Treasures of the Pacific Northwest
Buried Treasures of New England
Buried Treasures of the Atlantic Coast
Buried Treasures of the Mid-Atlantic States
New Mexico Treasure Tales
Colorado Treasure Tales
Lost Mines and Buried Treasures of Arizona
Lost Mines and Buried Treasures of Old Wyoming
Lost Mines and Buried Treasures of Arkansas
Lost Mines and Buried Treasures of Missouri
Texas Tales of Lost Mines and Buried Treasures
Legend and Lore of the Guadalupe Mountains
Lost Mines and Buried Treasures of the Guadalupe Mountains
Lost Treasures in American History
Buried Treasures of the Ozarks and Appalachians
Outlaw Treasures (audio)
Buried Treasures of the Civil War (audio)

Beyond the Grave Series

Billy the Kid: Beyond the Grave
Billy the Kid: The Lost Interviews
The Return of the Assassin, John Wilkes Booth

Books on Writing

Hot Coffee and Cold Truth: Living and Writing the West
Notes From Texas: On Writing in the Lone Star State
Want to be a Successful Writer? Do This Stuff
An Elevated View: Colorado Writers on Writing

Poetry

I Missed the Train to Little Rock
Open Range: Poetry of the Re-imagined West
   (Edited With Laurie Wagner Buyer)

Food

Chili from the Southwest
The Ultimate Chili Cookbook

Fiction

Beating the Devil

Other

Unsolved Mysteries of the Old West
A Sense of Place: Essays on the Ozarks
Ozark Tales of Ghosts, Spirits, Hauntings, and Monsters

Table of Contents

Introduction	vii
Lost Dalton Gang Loot	1
Lost California Gold in the Osage Hills	7
Belle Starr's Mystery Treasure	15
The Lost Treasure of Chief Blackface	23
Buzzard Hill Treasure	31
The Lost Gold Ingots of the Renegade Priest	35
Flat Top Mountain Treasure	43
Outlaw Bill Cook's Lost Treasure Cache	51
Lost Gold Coin Cache in Sequoyah County	57
Spanish Treasure in Tulsa	63
Outlaw Coin Cache	69
Creek Indian Settlement Treasure	79
Harmony Gold Coin Cache	83
Joseph Payne's Lost Vein of Silver	87
Jesse James Gold Cache in the Wichita Mountains	93
The Lost Army Payroll	99
Lost Mormon Gold Mine in the Spavinaw Hills	107
Lost Spanish Treasure in the Wichita Mountains	113
Lost Mexican Gold Ingots	121
The Cobbler's Gold Cache	129
The Buried Military Gold Shipment	135

Devil's Canyon Gold	143
A Word About Sources	153
About the Author	154

Introduction

The name Oklahoma is derived from two Choctaw Indian words: *Okla*, which means red, and *homma*, which means people. Indeed, between the forced resettling of a number of the plains tribes such as Cheyenne, Comanche, Arapaho, Pawnee, Osage, Wichita, Caddo, and Kiowa into this area, along with making it a destination for Cherokee, Choctaw, Chickasaw, Creek, and Seminoles Indians removed from the American South and East during the 1820s, Oklahoma was primarily a land of red people for a long time. In fact, before it received its official name, the region was formally known as Indian Territory. Today, representatives of sixty different tribes reside in Oklahoma.

Oklahoma was visited by European explorers during the sixteenth century. In 1541, Francisco Vasquez de Coronado crossed western Oklahoma on his way to Kansas. Why? He was in search of gold, having been lured to the area by Indian legends of cities constructed of the precious metal. Around this time, another Spaniard, Hernando de Soto, is believed by some to have ventured into Oklahoma. Among his objectives were to locate deposits of precious metal. In

1682, the French explorer LaSalle visited this area and claimed it for France as part of the land they called Louisiana. In 1762, France ceded Louisiana to Spain, but it was reclaimed by Napoleon in 1800. The United States purchased Oklahoma in 1803, but statehood did not arrive until November 16, 1907.

During the late 1880s, lands heretofore reserved for Indians were opened up to white settlers. In a short time, vast fields of wheat were springing from the broad plains that only years earlier saw native grasses and immense herds of bison. Today, in addition to agriculture, Oklahoma boasts impressive production of gas and oil.

In addition to petroleum, Oklahoma has historically seen the mining of gold and silver over the years. During some of the early Spanish forays into the region, gold and silver was discovered and mining was undertaken on a comparatively large scale. Mining was made difficult, however, because most of the activity occurred in tradition Indian homelands. The threat of hostile Indians who resented the trespass was constant, and on numerous occasion miners were driven out.

Years passed, and with the Spanish gone from this area and from Mexico, Mexicans arrived from south of the border to reopen a number of the gold and silver mines that had been earlier worked by their ancestors. The amount of ore taken from such mines amounted to many millions of dollars, but these were closed down and covered over for a variety of reasons. Many are still searched for today.

In addition to Indians, miners, farmers, and ranchers, Oklahoma saw the arrival of outlaws, men anxious to pluck riches from the prosperous and income from the growing towns and communities. Many bank and stagecoach robberies ended up with the loot being cached, the outlaws captured or killed, and the booty, often in gold and silver coins, never found. Ever surfacing clues continued to lure treasure hunters.

The numerous tales and legends related to lost mines and buried treasures in Oklahoma are often supported by documentation. The stories included in this book are most compelling because they offer chances of recovery. Though obscured by the passage of many decades since they were originally hidden or lost, these elusive treasures nevertheless continue to tempt the adventurous, the committed, the passionate. The quest remains alive.

Lost Dalton Gang Loot

The five men rode in silence along the narrow trail. Each of them scanned the surroundings in the moonlit darkness, ever on the alert for the presence of others who might be lawmen. At every strange sound, the riders would pause, listen, and, once determining there was no threat, continue. It was October 5, 1892.

The men were veterans of the outlaw trail, having pursued their living by robbing travelers, trains, and banks. The objective of this journey was to rob two banks at the same time in Coffeyville, Kansas: The First National Bank and the C. M. Condon and Company Bank. Never before in history had two banks been robbed at the same time by the same men. It was a bold plan, but the riders were used to taking risks.

They rode in the woods that bordered the Verdigris River in the Cherokee Nation, four miles south of the tiny village of Nowata in northeastern Oklahoma. This was a strip of lawless land. Lawmen hesitated to enter the region, and many who did were never seen again. Still, it paid to be on the alert. Several rewards had been offered for their capture or killing, rewards totaling well into the thousands of dollars.

The group had rendezvoused days earlier near Tulsa, some eighty miles south of the present location, to finalize their plans. After successfully taking all of the cash and gold at two Coffeeville banks, the outlaws intended to head for Mexico. If everything went as planned, they would flee Coffeeville and hasten to a location where Amos Burton, a black man, awaited with a covered wagon. The riders would don disguises, dressing themselves as women, and Burton would drive them south through Texas and thence into Mexico where they intended to live on the proceeds of the Coffeeville robberies along with other loot they had accumulated. Weeks earlier, the gang had stopped and robbed a Missouri, Kansas, and Texas train near Wagner, Oklahoma, and another MKT train near Adair.

A week after the Adair robbery, the gang walked into a bank in El Reno, Oklahoma, and robbed it of $17,000. After living high for several weeks, purchasing clothes, horses, and fine Mexican saddles, there remained $9,000 in gold and silver coins. Their saddlebags sagged under the weight of the loot as the outlaws rode toward Coffeeville.

The five men comprised what lawmen called the Dalton Gang, consisting of Emmett, Bob, and Grat Dalton along with friends Dick Broadwell and Bill Powers. At the time, the Dalton Gang was regarded as the most notorious outlaw band in the West. Emmett, the leader, rode in front. The remaining outlaws rode two abreast. Each wore brand new clothes and each sat in brand new Mexican saddles purchased especially for this escapade.

At 3:00 a.m. on the morning of October 6, the five men rode onto the farm of P. L. Davis a short distance from the Oklahoma-Kansas border not far from present-day South Coffeeville, Oklahoma. After making their way across a freshly plowed field, they entered a thicket of scrub oak on the west bank of Onion Creek, a tributary of the Verdigris River.

Here, they set up camp, built a small fire, and boiled some coffee. Two of the riders rode to a nearby cornfield on the J. F. Savage farm and harvested some of the grain for the horses.

Following a short, simple meal, the riders curled up in their bedrolls for a bit of sleep. Their rest was short, for they rose just before dawn. During a breakfast of hardboiled eggs, biscuits, and coffee, Emmett Dalton decided that the weight of the gold and silver in their saddlebags would work to their disadvantage in the event that they might have to outrun pursuing lawmen. The coins were removed and buried nearby on the bank of Onion Creek. Following the robberies of the two Coffeeville banks, the outlaws intended to return to the location, retrieve the buried loot, and continue on to the rendezvous with Amos Burton.

As the Dalton Gang buried the coins near the creek not far from a wooden bridge, the sun was only minutes from rising. At the same time, a young girl, the daughter of farmer James Brown, saddled her mare and left for an early morning ride.

As she neared the wooden bridge spanning Onion Creek, the girl was surprised to see five men ride out from under it and proceed down the road toward Coffeeville. They did not see her as they galloped toward the north. Several weeks later when the young girl learned about the Dalton Gang and the Coffeeville bank robbery, she realized that, had she followed the tracks of the five men when they were fresh, she might have come upon a sizeable cache of wealth.

It was 9:30 a.m. when the Dalton Gang rode into Coffeeville. They rode slowly down the main street and stopped in front of the home of a policeman named Munn where they dismounted and hitched their horses. The five men wore slickers that bulged in the middle from the firearms they carried. They set out on foot toward the two banks.

The outlaws were not expecting trouble, but the citizens of Coffeeville were. Aware that the Dalton Gang was on its way to their town, armed men waited in hiding behind anything that offered shelter. Inside the banks, the outlaws managed to stuff a total of $20,000 into canvas sacks before deciding it was time to leave. It was at that moment that dozens of men opened fire on the escaping outlaws.

Within twelve minutes, Grat and Bob Dalton, along with Bill Powers, had been killed. Emmett lay on the ground, bleeding from twenty-three rifle bullets in his body. Dick Broadwell managed to reach his horse, mount it, and spur it back toward Onion Creek. Shot before he could get out of town, Broadwell managed to remain in the saddle for another quarter of a mile before falling to the ground, dead.

During the melee, the Dalton Gang killed four Coffeeville citizens. Three others were seriously wounded. The entire $20,000 was recovered along with some cash found in the pockets of the outlaws.

While his wounds were being treated, Emmett Dalton told the doctor that the gang had left Tulsa, Oklahoma, with $9,000 in gold and silver coins in their saddlebags. When pressed for details about where the money might be, Emmett refused to say any more. When he was told that the rest of his gang had been killed and that he was not expected to live, Emmett clung to his story.

The dead bandits were quickly buried in Coffeeville's Elmwood Cemetery. Many wondered about the reasons for the hasty burial. A rumor spread through town that large sums of money had been sewed into the linings of the outlaw's clothes. A number of citizens wanted to dig up the bodies for a closer look, but it was not permitted.

In spite of his wounds, Emmett Dalton survived. Following a trial, he was found guilty and sentenced to prison for life. After fifteen years behind bars, however, he was granted a pardon. Following his release, Emmett was closely watched in the belief that he would eventually lead investigators to the buried loot. Emmett Dalton surprised them all by settling down to a rather quiet and peaceful life.

It is a fact that Emmett Dalton returned to the region of Onion Creek on several occasions, but as far as is known he never dug up any of the cached gold and silver coins.

Most researchers concur that the $9,000 in gold and silver coins in 1892 values is still buried near Onion Creek in Nowata County near the location of the old wooden bridge that spanned the stream. If found today, the estimated value of the loot is placed at nearly $200,000.

The cache could bring more. In recent years, Dalton-related relics and memorabilia have been bringing high prices among collectors. Even the headstone from the Daltons' grave has been stolen and, it was believed, sold to a collector.

Lost Mines and Buried Treasures of Oklahoma

W. C. Jameson

Lost California Gold in the Osage Hills

The horse-drawn wagons creaked and sagged under the weight of the gold and supplies they were transporting. They moved slow and southward across the dry, dusty Kansas prairie. The drivers of the wagons, along with the six men on horseback accompanying them, were returning to their Missouri homes following years of panning and digging gold in the Sierra Nevada Mountains of California. They estimated they had accumulated a total of $100,000 in the valuable ore, an impressive fortune for the day, and one that would be worth many millions at today's values. The year was 1862.

The men were making their way along a stretch of trail that travelers called the California Road. It was one of dozens that webbed through Kansas and Oklahoma during the gold rush days that saw thousands of eager and ambitious men journey to the Golden State to seek their fortunes. So many men and wagons had crossed this expanse of prairie that the road now consisted of deep ruts. The men in the wagons and on horseback did not care, for after many years of toil the road was taking them home.

Days earlier the travelers had broken camp outside the town of McPherson, Kansas, loaded the wagons, saddled their horses, packed the mules, and set out in a southerly direction toward Oklahoma, then referred to as Indian Territory. Unknown to the travelers, a band of Pawnees had been observing them from hiding in the nearby woods. The Indians eyed the horses ridden by the travelers and coveted the mounts and the mules for themselves. They were curious about what the wagons contained. The Indians were in need of cloth, cooking gear, and tools, and hoped they would find such in the vehicles.

When the wagons and riders disappeared over the horizon to the south, the Pawnees rode out of the woods and followed, keeping well behind. They would continue to watch the travelers and, when the time was right, they would attack.

Moving slow, the gold miners eventually left Kansas and entered Indian Territory, following the road as it veered southeastward passing north of the present-day town of Pawhuska. As the travelers followed the road into the Osage Hills located a few miles northeast of Pawhuska, The Indians left the trail and raced their horses in a wide detour that took them into a preselected valley in the hills. There, in hiding, they waited for the travelers to arrive.

One hour before sundown, the caravan entered the little valley. The Pawnees charged, screaming, from a nearby hill. The miners, unprepared for the attack, attempted to shield themselves behind the wagons. Surprised and panicked, they fired into the ranks of the Indians, but were ineffective. Time and again, arrows found their mark, and one by one the travelers fell to the ground, dead.

A miner who had been elected to the position of leader of the party realized there was little to no chance of surviving the onslaught. As he watched his companions die, his thoughts turned to escaping. During a lull in the brief battle, he loaded one of the mules with a portion of gold from a wagon. While the Pawnees were distracted by renewed firing from his companions, he led the gold-laden mule through the waist-high grass of the valley floor into a nearby copse of prairie oaks. Miraculously, he went unnoticed by the Indians.

When the fight resumed, the leader made his way through the trees and behind a low hill. An hour later, he found himself back on the trail that led to Missouri. While the Pawnees were rushing into the midst of the surviving miners, killing them all, the leader continued his trek toward home, now bearing a fortune in gold.

As the sun set, the Indians secured the surviving horses of the miners and rummaged through the contents of the wagons. Save for some camping items, they found little to interest them. The Pawnee had no interest in the metal so coveted by the white men and the gold nuggets were spilled out of the canvas sacks onto the ground. When the Indians had accumulated all of the plunder they wanted, they set fire to the wagons and rode away.

As they left the area, one of the warriors spotted the tracks of a man and a mule and realized that one of the travelers had escaped. That night the Indians set up camp near the burning wagons. In the morning, they would set out in pursuit of the remaining traveler.

The miner walked all night leading the mule carrying his fortune in gold. Travel was difficult, for the load was significant, and even the stout mule began to stagger under such a burden after many hours.

When daylight arrived the next morning, the traveler continued his journey, but was slowed by the now fatigued mule. Time and again he looked down the trail behind him to make certain he was not being pursued. Just after noon he encountered a small spring at which he paused to water himself and the mule. Nearby was an aged tree with a hollow cavity. As the mule drank, the traveler stared back down the trail and spotted the Indians a few miles behind. They were following his tracks and would be upon him in no time.

Concerned that he would not be able to escape or hide as long as he had the mule, he decided to bury the gold and return for it later. He scooped out a shallow trench in the prairie earth, deposited the bags of gold ore, and covered them. Leaving his mule, he walked to the nearby tree and placed his rifle in the hollow. Taking quick note of his surroundings, he fled on foot, hoping the Indians would be happy to retrieve the mule and leave him alone. Luck was with him, for he saw no more of the Pawnees.

Weeks later, the traveler arrived at his home in Missouri where he was greeted by his wife and son. It required more weeks for him to recover from his ordeal, and while he was recuperating, he related the story of the wagons filled with gold, the attack by the Pawnees, and his escape.

When he was asked when he planned to return for the gold, the miner replied that he would not venture back into the wild region of Indian Territory for all the gold in the world. Referring to his son, he told others that when grown and the threat of Indian attack had diminished he could go look for the cache.

As he was recovering, the traveler sketched a map and jotted down vague directions relative to the location of the attack by the Pawnees in the Osage Hills and the place near the spring where he buried the mule load of gold. Researchers familiar with this tale have placed the approximate location of the spring south of a landmark known as Artillery Hill, and between a branch of the California Road and the Caney River that flows into

Oklahoma out of Kansas. He gave the directions to his wife. Twenty years later, she passed them on to their son.

When he was able to allocate the time, the son decided to set off in search of the treasure in gold buried by his father. Following the directions originally penned and sketched by his late father, he arrived at what he was convinced was the correct vicinity. The location was on an Osage County farm owned by an Osage Indian named Joe Boulanger.

The son approached Boulanger and told him what he was searching for. The two men agreed to look for the buried treasure together. Boulanger was certain he knew the precise location of the spring where the father had stopped to water himself and the mule, where he buried the gold, and where he hid the rifle in the hollow of an old tree.

Boulanger recalled, as a child, hearing about one of the neighbors finding an old rifle in a tree out near the spring. The verification of this part of the story encouraged the two men. The tree, along with several others located near the spring, however, had long since been cut down during a period when they were expanding the limits of the pasture. The spring had dried up, but Boulanger was certain he could relocate it.

Boulanger and the son encountered several locations that could have once been a spring. Though they dug holes in a number of likely locations, they were never able to locate any buried gold. After two weeks of searching and finding nothing, the son discontinued his search and returned to his farm in Missouri. He never made another trip to northeastern Oklahoma to search for his father's buried gold. It is assumed that the mule load of gold, likely worth well over one million dollars today, still lies a few inches under the surface near the old spring.

And what of the gold that remained on the wagons attacked by the Pawnees in the Osage Hills? Chances are it still lies on the ground in the small valley that was the site of the massacre. An event occurred during the 1970s that renewed interest in the two wagons filled with California gold.

The Osage Hills are now a state park. During a weekend in 1978, a family consisting of parents and two children, a boy and a girl, were hiking in an area of the Osage Hills that was some distance away from the prescribed trails. As they explored through the pleasant region, the son handed his father a metal fitting that was identified as having once been part of a wagon. Searching around the area, the father and son found more artifacts including wagon bolts, wheel rims, bridle bits, and more. In all, according to the father, about four or five bucket loads of scraps were located, all of them from wagons or gear from saddle horses.

Because they were hiking in an area where they were not supposed to be, the father did not relate his discovery to any of the state park officials. Weeks later, however, after explaining his discovery to an acquaintance, he was informed of the tale of the gold-filled wagons that had been attacked by the Pawnee Indians in 1862 and the fortune that had remained lost ever since.

Enthused by the notion that he was only inches away from finding the gold and becoming wealthy, the father returned to the park two weeks later and attempted to relocate the small valley where the artifacts were encountered. He was never able to find it. Though he searched the region off and on for two years, he could not find the specific valley where the metal artifacts were found.

The gold ore still lies on the ground in a seldom-visited valley in the Osage Hills. Based on the information provided by the surviving miner and handed down over the years in his family, it is likely that millions of dollars worth of the nuggets lay scattered across the limited area where the massacre occurred.

Belle Starr's Mystery Treasure

The outlaw Belle Starr was a fascinating mix of truth and myth and it is sometimes difficult for the researcher to discern where one ends and the other begins. It is well known that Starr, one of America' most famous female outlaws, was a horse thief and consorted with other outlaws known to rob banks and trains, among them Frank and Jesse James and the Younger Gang.

One of the most curious tales associated with Starr involves the robbery of a shipment of United States Government gold from a train and the subsequent caching of the gold in a cave in the Wichita Mountains of south-central Oklahoma. Some researchers have insisted that the event never occurred, but evidence that has accumulated over the years suggests otherwise.

It has been alleged that sometime during the mid-1880s, Belle Starr and her gang stopped a train bearing a cargo of federal U.S. gold ingots bound for the Denver Mint. The outlaws encountered no resistance and the robbery went smoothly. Fearing pursuit from federal lawmen, however, Starr decided to cache the gold until things cooled down. She selected a cave located in the Wichita Mountains in which to hide the loot, one she had passed several times during her travels. Just before riding away from the scene of the robbery, one of the gang members removed the iron door to a boxcar. The outlaws attached ropes to the door and dragged it along behind them into the mountain range. Once the gold had been placed in the cave, the iron door was fitted over the opening, secured with an intricate lock, and partially covered with rock and brush.

During a subsequent train robbery attempt several months later, all of the members of Starr's gang were allegedly killed. In 1889, Belle was mysteriously murdered, a crime that has never been solved. With her death, no one remained alive who knew the precise location of what has subsequently been termed Belle Starr's Lost Iron Door Cache.

Over time, investigators for the railroad learned of the possible existence of the cache in the Wichita Mountains and, though they searched for months, were never able to locate it. More time passed, and the incident occupied less of the detectives' time. Eventually it was forgotten altogether.

Two decades after the train robbery and the caching of the gold, an area rancher and his son were riding through a portion of the Wichita Mountains on their way to the home of some friends in the tiny town of Indiahoma on the south side of the range. The pair got a late start and, hoping to reach their destination before nightfall, took an unfamiliar shortcut. The trail passed alongside Elk Mountain and wound through a deep canyon. As the sun was setting, a bright reflection from a canyon wall caught the attention of the riders. On investigating, the father and son found a large, rusted iron boxcar door set into a recessed area along the canyon wall. The boy wanted to investigate further, but the father was determined to reach the home of their friends before nightfall. He promised the boy they would return another day and try to discover what lay behind the iron door.

When the two arrived at their destination, they related their experience to the host, describing the iron door they had spotted on one side of the canyon. The host grew excited and related the story of Belle Starr's train robbery and the caching of a fortune in gold. Intrigued, the father decided that during their return the next morning they would investigate the iron door.

The father and son breakfasted, saddled their mounts, and were on the trail by sunrise, retracing the trail they had taken the day before. They entered the canyon in which they believed they had found the iron door, but on this trip were unable to relocate it. Up and down the canyon they rode in search of the iron door, but as the day wore on and they had no success, they decided to return home. The father and son made a number of trips into the same canyon during the following years, but each time their search for the iron door was unsuccessful.

The father and son even explored other nearby canyons, but their quest always remained futile. In time, the father was convinced that one had to be in a certain location at a specific time of the day in order to see the rays of sunlight reflecting off of the metal railroad door. In spite of years of searching, they never found themselves in the right canyon at the appropriate time. Eventually, they gave up their quest.

Around the time the father and son discovered the iron door in the remote canyon in the Wichita range, an elderly woman arrived in the area following a long, tiresome journey from Missouri. The woman introduced herself as Mrs. Holt and had in her possession a map that purportedly showed the location of Belle Starr's iron door cache. Mrs.

Holt also displayed a large key that she claimed would unlock the door.

Mrs. Holt explained that years earlier she had treated the wounds of a dying outlaw who claimed to have been a member of Belle Starr's gang that robbed the train and hid the gold in the cave. Before dying, the outlaw sketched a crude map showing the location of the cave and describing the iron door set over the entrance. He also gave her the key that he said would unlock it. At one point he explained that there was a large tree not far from the cave that had a railroad spike hammered into the trunk. During the 1950s, a tree matching that description was identified. A few years later it was cut down, and no one remained alive who could remember its exact location.

In 1910, a group of four teenagers was exploring a remote canyon in the Wichita range when they encountered the iron door. One of the boys provided a detailed description of the door and the large rusted padlock that held it shut. The boys assumed the cave was being used by a local rancher to store supplies, so they left it alone. Two decades later, one of the youths heard the story of the lost iron door cache. Now a grown man with a family, he returned many times to what he was convinced was the same canyon but he was never able to relocate the iron door. He stated that the canyon was located just to the north of Treasure Lake, the same general area identified by the man and his son years earlier.

During the 1920s, a group of coon hunters entered the Wichita Mountains with their hunting dogs. They established a campsite in a canyon and set about searching for game. At one point their dogs treed a raccoon. As one of the hunters was taking aim at the animal, he was distracted by a reflection from the opposite canyon wall. Curious, he climbed to the top of a nearby boulder and, using binoculars, attempted to determine the origin of the reflection. He determined that it was coming from a large piece of metal set in a recessed portion of the canyon wall.

The coon hunter wanted to investigate the anomalous object, but his companions insisted they continue with their hunting, stating they would return another day. Weeks later they arrived in the canyon to have a closer look at the metal object but were unable to find it. These men, like others before them, claimed the door was spotted in a canyon near Treasure Lake.

Several years later, three boys were hiking through the Wichita Mountains to Indiahoma. Since they were in a hurry, they decided to cut through a canyon they believed would save them some time. The trek along the canyon floor led them past a large rusty iron railroad door set into the mountainside. The boys climbed to the door and inspected it and the big lock that held it shut. They tried to pry the door open in order to see what was behind it but were unsuccessful. Unaware of the great fortune in gold that lay just beyond the door, the three boys gave up and continued on with their journey.

Fifty years later, one of the boys learned the story of Belle Starr's Iron Door Cache. Convinced it was located where he and his friends once encountered the rusted railroad door in the remote canyon, he decided to return to the area to try to relocate it. Like all of the others before him, his attempt was a failure. All he could remember at the time was that the canyon was located not far from Treasure Lake.

Lost Mines and Buried Treasures of Oklahoma

* * *

In 1932, an itinerant farm worker was walking from Hobart to Lawton to look for work. His route took him through the Wichita Mountains. At nightfall, he stopped at the entrance of a canyon, built a fire, prepared supper, then wrapped himself in his blanket and went to sleep. The following morning he resumed his journey, the trail taking him past Elk Mountain. During his hike, he explained weeks later, he passed what he described as a rust-stained iron door barely seen on the mountainside.

The farm worker was somewhat familiar with the story of the iron door cache and was convinced he had located it. He climbed to the door and struggled for a long time to try to open it. He removed a great many rocks and boulders and cleared away brush but was unable to gain entry; he determined that it would require heavy tools. On arriving in the next town, he enlisted the help of two men who supplied the necessary tools along with some dynamite. When they returned to the canyon, however, the door could not be found. They searched all day, retracing their steps many times, but were unable to relocate it.

An Oklahoma resident named Stephens revealed that he had found the door during the 1940s. He claimed he was hiking in a canyon near Treasure Lake when he spotted the object set in a shallow recess in the canyon wall and not far from the trail. He accurately described an old boxcar door from the 1880s and said it was partially concealed by rocks and brush. He attempted to pry the door open but was unable to budge it. He decided to return later with some tools to assist him in opening the door. As he was leaving the canyon, he constructed a cairn of rocks at a trail crossing to help him identify the exact route when he returned. Several weeks later Stephens, in the company of several men and a wagon transporting tools, was unable to relocate the cairn or the canyon.

In recent years, hikers who have returned from exploring a remote canyon near Treasure Lake reported seeing a large iron door set against one wall. Unfamiliar with the story of Belle Starr's Iron Door Cache, they returned home and resumed their normal activities, unaware they may have passed within a few feet of several million dollars worth of gold.

The search for Belle Starr's Iron Door Cache continues. In 1994 a man returned from a day long hike in a remote canyon near Elk Mountain, a hike during which he took several dozen photographs. On having them developed, he noticed on one particular shot of some flowers near a canyon wall was the unmistakable image of a rusted metal boxcar door several feet beyond.

W. C. Jameson

The Lost Treasure of Chief Blackface

The line of mules snaked along a winding trail as it entered a portion of the Ozark Mountains not far from the present-day town of Tahlequah. To the front and rear of the mule train rode fourteen men, each one on the alert for bandits. From time to time, the leader of the group rode back along the line of mules, inspecting the loads transported by each one of them, and making certain they were secure. Should they be forced into a running escape, he did not want to risk losing any of the packs, for they contained millions of dollars worth of gold ore.

The year was 1836, and the riders, all Mexican, were traveling from the rich gold fields far to the west in Colorado. They were on their way to St. Louis, Missouri, where some of the gold would be traded for supplies and fresh mounts. The rest would be loaded onto a boat and transported down the Mississippi to the Gulf of Mexico and thence to Vera Cruz where relatives would be waiting to receive it. Their route took them south of the Kansas plains and into Oklahoma in the hope of avoiding hostile Indian tribes. It was not to be. Once the miners were resupplied and well rested, they intended to return to their mines and harvest even more of the precious metal.

As the Mexicans made their way into the realm of mountains and canyons, a Cherokee Indian was spurring his mount toward the campsite of Chief Blackface. An hour earlier, the Indian spotted the mule train and its well-armed escort. Convinced the pack train was carrying items of value, he hastened to alert the notorious Chief Blackface. Should a subsequent raid on the mule train yield riches, the rider knew he would be rewarded with a portion of it as he had many times in the past.

Blackface was the offspring of a Cherokee mother and an African, a former slave who made his way to Indian Territory and took up residence with the tribe. By the time he was twenty years old, Blackface had assembled a gang of cutthroats that made their living attacking and robbing travelers, homesteaders, and anyone else unlucky enough to be caught on the trails in his range. More often than not, the robbery victims were left dead on the trail

Blackface was called chief by the white settlers in the area, though no such distinction was ever awarded him by his tribe. Blackface was an outlaw and a killer, nothing more.

Knowing which route the pack train had to take to make its way through the range, Blackface led his gang to an area through which they must pass. It was a narrow canyon, one in which it would be easy to trap and slay all of the members of the pack train's escort.

Two hours after the Indians had settled into their hiding places, the Mexicans and the mule train entered the canyon. At the appropriate time, Blackface screamed a signal. Seconds later a dozen Cherokees streamed from their hiding places and charged into the unsuspecting miners, firing arrows and hurling lances as they rode. One of the first to fall was a young Mexican named Estévez. Badly wounded, he crawled unnoticed behind a jumble of rocks where he watched as his companions were slaughtered by the Indians.

Within a few short minutes the remaining miners were dead. As some of the Indians took rifles and pistols from the corpses, others removed boots and other articles of clothing they desired. Blackface inspected the packs carried by the mules. He found mining tools, camping equipment, and molds for making bullets. To his surprise and delight, he found several packs filled with gold, the precious metal so prized by the white men. The Cherokee had little use for gold other than fashioning ornaments such as armbands. Blackface, however, was aware of the white man's passion and lust for this strange metal and knew that it could be used to trade for weapons, ammunition, and fine horses.

For the time being, however, Blackface decided it would be necessary to hide the gold in a location he could easily return to when it was needed. After rounding up the horses of the dead Mexicans, Blackface and his men led the gold-laden mules to a remote cave in the nearby mountains. There, the ore-filled packs were unloaded and stacked against the back wall of the cave.

After Blackface and his gang departed, young Estévez crept from his hiding place. Assured he was not being observed, the youth stumbled out of the canyon and, after the passage of many months, made his way back to his home in Mexico where he described the killing of his countrymen and the theft of the gold.

From time to time over the years, Blackface and a few chosen warriors would return to the cave, remove some of the gold, and use it purchase items needed by the gang. More often than not, however, more gold and other treasure was added to the hoard as a result of additional robberies.

At one point, it was estimated that Blackface had access to millions of dollars worth of gold, currency, and other wealth in his secret cave.

A number of law enforcement agencies in this portion of the Ozark Mountains of eastern Oklahoma were interested in seeing Chief Blackface's reign of terror ended. Citizens lived in fear of the Indian and his gang and wanted him captured and hung. In addition, the Cherokee tribal police were after him.

As Blackface and his gang grew bolder, efforts to capture or kill him were intensified. Many believed it was just a matter of time before the Indian outlaw was put out of business. Following weeks of tracking the gang, a contingent of Cherokee police finally caught up with them. Following a brief gun battle, Blackface and all of his followers were killed. With their death went the knowledge of the location of the secret treasure cave.

For years after the death of Chief Blackface, residents in this part of the Oklahoma Ozarks wondered about the location of the treasure cave. Now and again, a few would set out in search if it, but all returned unsuccessful.

One day during the 1930s, an elderly Cherokee Indian walked into the town of Tahlequah and, counting out a few coins from a weathered leather pouch, paid for a room in a local boarding house. Every morning, the Cherokee would leave the boarding house at dawn and walk into the nearby mountains. Each day he returned at sundown in time for dinner. One evening as he was dining, he became engaged in a conversation with the owner of the boarding house. He told the proprietor that he was searching for a treasure in gold ore that his ancestors had spoken of for many generations.

Weeks passed, and the old Cherokee was running out of money. He asked for a meeting with the owner of the boarding house and explained that he believed he was close to locating the secret treasure cave of Chief Blackface. He told the owner, a man named Smith, that if he would allow him to remain at the boarding house for a few more days, that he would provide him with a portion of the treasure. Smith agreed to allow the Indian to stay for another month.

Late one evening almost one month later, the Indian returned from the nearby mountains and entered the boarding house. He signaled to Smith that he needed to talk with him. Excusing himself from the other boarders, Smith led the Cherokee into an adjacent room. Breathlessly, the old man explained that he had finally found the treasure cave and that he would take Smith to it on the morrow.

Early the next morning following breakfast, the two men left the boarding house and hiked into the nearby mountains. After traveling for three miles, the Cherokee told Smith that from this point on he must be blindfolded. This done, he led him in a series of circles then set out on a rough trail. Three hours later, the two men were standing in front of a cave. Leaving the blindfold on Smith, the Cherokee bent to the task of removing some of the stones that covered the entrance to the cave. Twenty minutes later, the Indian, breathing heavily, told Smith that he would now lead him into the cave.

For the first dozen yards, the two men had to stoop to avoid hitting the ceiling, but presently arrived at a location where they could stand upright. In the dim light from the entrance, the Cherokee gathered some dry wood, started a fire, and fashioned a torch. With Smith still blindfolded, the Indian led him deeper into the cave for another few dozen years. Pausing here, the Indian removed the blindfold.

Inviting Smith to observe, the Cherokee walked around the small chamber holding the torch above his head to illuminate the space. Stacked against one wall, he saw several leather packs. The Cherokee opened one of them and gold nuggets spilled out onto the floor. A short distance away rested six clay pots, each one filled to the top with small gold ingots. Smith calculated that it would take nearly fifteen mules to transport all of the gold he saw lying in the cave.

Realizing he was in the presence of a fortune worth millions of dollars, Smith proposed to the Cherokee that he would organize a small group of trustworthy acquaintances, secure some mules, and return to the cave, remove the treasure, and divide it.

The old Cherokee thought in silence for several minutes, and then responded. He told Smith that before any of the treasure could be removed, the appropriate Cherokee rituals must be conducted. He stated that this was necessary in order to remove any curses that might have been placed on the treasure and the cave. He asked for a few days to accomplish this. Reluctantly, Smith agreed. He did not want to jeopardize this opportunity to become wealthy beyond his dreams.

Before leaving, the Cherokee told Smith that he could take two of the small gold bars. After the tiny ingots were placed in his pockets, Smith was again blindfolded by the Indian and led out of the cave. Though blindfolded, Smith was aware that a different route was followed back to Tahlequah. The two men arrived at the boarding house after sundown. The Cherokee bade Smith goodnight and said he would begin the Indian rituals in the morning. Smith was already counting his fortune and imagining what it would buy.

The following morning arrived and the Cherokee did not come down for breakfast. When Smith checked the room, he noted that the Indian was not there and his bed had not been slept in. Elements of a panic began to grow in Smith as he imagined the opportunities for recovering the fortune in gold vanishing.

Later that day, Smith learned that instead of going straight to bed, the Indian had gone into town and gotten into a fight with one of Tahlequah's citizens. During the melee, the old Indian stabbed his opponent several times and the victim was not expected to live. The Cherokee was nowhere to be found. A search for the Indian was undertaken but he was never seen again.

Smith returned to the nearby hills many times to try to locate the secret treasure cave. When he began to doubt that he had actually seen the treasure, he would withdraw the two small gold bars he was allowed to retrieve and regarded them for many long minutes. The treasure was real, and he resolved to find it.

Smith searched for the treasure cave for years but his quest was fruitless. Eventually, he gave up. Over the years, others have entered the hills and mountains near Tahlequah in search of Chief Blackface's lost treasure cave, but none were successful. If found today, it is estimated that the treasure would be worth in excess of twenty million dollars.

Lost Mines and Buried Treasures of Oklahoma

Buzzard Hill Treasure

As indicated by the previous tale, the relationship between lost treasure and Mexicans has been a long-standing one in Oklahoma. The truth is, the presence of Mexicans, as well as the Spaniards before them, was not uncommon in the area, and much of it was related to mining precious metals. Abundant evidence for this has been found numerous times over the past several decades.

During the mid-eighteenth century, a group of nine Mexicans was mining gold from a granite outcrop in the foothills of the Ouachita Mountains located not far from the present-day town of Spiro in LeFlore County. The area was sparsely settled during this time, and the Mexicans conducted their activities in relative solitude.

Over a period of several weeks when the miners had accumulated a significant amount of the ore, they would load it onto mules and transport it a short distance out of the hills to the north across the floodplain to a location on the Arkansas River. Here, the gold was loaded onto a raft and floated eastward down the river through Arkansas to the Mississippi River and thence on to New Orleans. At the Crescent City, the gold ore was traded for coin and supplies. The bulk of the coins were shipped to families in

Mexico. Once resupplied, the Mexicans returned to their mine in Oklahoma.

This routine continued for many years and involved at least two generations of the miners. In time, the French, who claimed this territory until the Louisiana Purchase of 1803, had observed the Mexicans in New Orleans exchanging their gold and grew curious about its origin. Over a period of two more years, the French learned of the existence of the gold mine in the Ouachita Mountains. Once this was determined, they sent a force of soldiers and laborers to evict the Mexicans and take over the mining operations.

The Mexicans learned of the impending arrival of and takeover by the French, who were still weeks away. They decided they would abandon the mine and return to Mexico for a time. While there, they would remain apprised of the activities of the French and, when the time was right, return to the area and resume their mining activities.

The miners gathered up all of the gold ore they had accumulated and buried it nearby. They placed all of their tools and other equipment inside the mine, sealed the entrance with rocks, and covered it to make it such appear to be part of the surrounding area. This done, they undertook the long overland journey back to Mexico.

The miners' trip back to their homeland was not uneventful. On several occasions they were attacked by Indians. Six of them were killed as a result. With the passage of more time, the three survivors were never able to bring themselves to organize another expedition to the gold mine so far away in the north. Eventually, the matter was forgotten.

The existence of the rich gold mine came to light in 1861 when a stranger arrived at the town of Spiro. The newcomer, a Mexican, asked a number of questions pertaining to certain landmarks and was soon directed to a ranch located a short distance north of town. On arriving, the Mexican introduced himself to the rancher and explained the reason for his visit.

The Mexican related the story of the rich gold mine located nearby, the decades of mining undertaken by his ancestors, and the riches taken from it. He explained how, prior to abandoning the area, the mine entrance was hidden and the accumulated gold ore buried somewhere close. He told the rancher he wished to enter into an agreement wherein he would be able to reopen the mine, resume mining operations, and share the profits.

The rancher was skeptical and asked a number of questions. He learned that the mine was located at a place the Mexican referred to as *La Loma del Zopilote*, Spanish for Buzzard Hill. When the rancher said there was no such place, the Mexican told him that was how it was referred to by the miners. The Mexican further explained that he had in his possession a map that would lead them to the precise location of the mine and the buried gold.

The rancher resisted the Mexican's offer. He was convinced that he would be able to locate the gold mine on his own and not have to share any of the wealth with his visitor. He told the Mexican to leave his property immediately and not return. Without a word the Mexican departed and was never seen in the area again. The rancher searched for the lost gold mine for years with no success. Eventually, he gave up.

The story of the Mexican gold mine at Buzzard Hill was all but forgotten until 1968 when a cache of a few mining tools and rusted camp gear was located near a granite outcrop not far from Spiro. As a result, interest in the long lost mine was revived and a few searches were undertaken. To date, however, it has not been found.

The Lost Gold Ingots of the Renegade Priest

Padre LaFarge was a native of France. Though he held the position of a priest for a time, his heart was that of an outlaw. In time he was to become responsible for the caching of what may be one of the richest lost treasures in the United States.

As a young man, LaFarge had been admitted to the priesthood in France and, when deemed ready, was sent to Mexico. There, LaFarge encountered little but trouble, most of it of his own doing. He was convicted of killing a nun, defrocked, and sent to prison. Several years later when he was released, LaFarge re-donned his priestly garb and re-assumed the role of a holy man. Unknown to the church, LaFarge conducted services, baptized babies, and married couples.

LaFarge's travels took him north and across the Rio Grande into Texas and New Mexico. Traveling from settlement to settlement, LaFarge used his disguise to advantage, convincing believers they would earn their place in heaven if they provided him with meals and a place to stay.

In time, LaFarge fell in with six other Frenchmen. With them, he traveled to Taos, New Mexico. Not far from the young and growing settlement, they established a gold placer mining operation along several of the small mountain streams found in the vicinity.

None of the Frenchmen had any mining experience and they soon grew frustrated with their efforts; the small amount of gold they gleaned from the streams was barely enough to purchase food and supplies in town.

The Frenchmen learned of a successful placer mining operation taking place in a nearby canyon, one conducted by a family of Mexicans. The Frenchmen decided it would be easier to take the gold from successful miners than to work for it themselves. A few days later, the seven men approached the Mexican miners, killed them all, and gathered up their gold.

Deciding this was an easier way to gain riches than the hard labor associated with panning gold, the Frenchmen located other placer mining operations, killed or drove away the miners, and took possession of the gold. Over the next several weeks, the Frenchmen killed twenty-two miners and accumulated so much gold they required several mules to transport it.

Deciding it would be more efficient to convert the gold ore into ingots, the Frenchmen hired a Spaniard named José Lopat. Lopat was experienced in smelting gold and casting it into ingots. By the time he was finished, he had fashioned five hundred bars from the ore supplied to him by the Frenchmen. The total weight of the gold was 4,000 pounds

LaFarge, who by now had assumed the role of leader of the group, ascertained it was time to quit the region before their deeds were discovered. After distributing the gold ingots and supplies into six oxcarts, the party left Taos and traveled along the old Santa Fe Trail. At some point, LaFarge intended to leave the trail and head toward New Orleans where they would book passage on a ship back to

France to live lives of luxury. Lopat hired on as guide, and six Indian slaves were purchased from a miner.

It was August, 1804, as the carts and riders entered the arid plains of what is now the Panhandle of Oklahoma. The oxen, tired and hungry as a result of long days and poor feed, plodded along the deep ruts of the trail. Covering the ingots in the carts were layers of furs. Anyone curious enough to look into the carts would assume the Frenchmen were trappers with a load of pelts heading for market.

LaFarge, who rode in the lead, scanned the horizon and was constantly on the lookout for Indians and bandits. The party was warned of an abundance of both in the area as they passed through small settlements along the way.

At one point o this part of the journey, Lopat, who had been scouting ahead, rode up to LaFarge and informed him he had located a spring a short distance ahead and, since it was only two hours until sundown, would serve as an appropriate place to set up camp for the night. Scanning the horizon for landmarks, LaFarge noted the presence of Sugar Loaf Mountain a few miles to the north.

Hours later, the expedition pulled up to what many researchers are convinced is Flagg Spring located in the north-central part of Cimarron County, the westernmost county in the Oklahoma Panhandle. Here they found four trappers already encamped, also transporting a load of furs. While LaFarge and his men were setting gathering firewood, the ex-priest engaged in conversation with the friendly trappers.

Perceiving no threat from the trappers, LaFarge told them about the cargo of gold ingots and of his plans to travel to New Orleans. The men informed LaFarge that the Crescent City no longer belonged to the French, that it had been sold to the United States. They cautioned LaFarge that there was a possibility the newly installed government of the United States would not permit him to ship the gold ingots out of the country. It was more likely, they explained, that the new government would confiscate the gold.

Following dinner, LaFarge held a meeting with his party. It was decided to send two of their number ahead to New Orleans to arrange for a vessel to meet them somewhere along the coast and far from the scrutiny of government agents. The next morning two of the Frenchmen mounted their horses and departed for New Orleans. Lafarge and the rest began to undertake arrangements to remain encamped at the spring until their companions returned. It was estimated it would take three-and-a-half months to make the round trip. LaFarge ordered the Indian slaves to get to work on the construction of several dugouts and rock dwellings for shelter against the approaching winter.

By the end of December, the two Frenchmen had not returned from their trip to New Orleans. LaFarge assumed something had befallen them and they would not be coming back. He decided to bury the gold bars until such time as he could determine the best way to have them delivered to France. Before burying the gold ingots, LaFarge ordered Lopat and the Indian slaves to return along the trail and wait for him in Santa Fe. Once they were out of sight, LaFarge and the remaining four Frenchman excavated a hole and buried the gold not far from the spring.

Weeks later and following his return to Santa Fe, Lopat learned of LaFarge's criminal past. Using blank pages at the back of his family Bible, Lopat wrote down what he had learned as well as his own role in converting the gold ore into ingots and helping transport it to the location at

Flagg Spring. It is this chronicle in the handwriting of Lopat that had provided most of the information about the buried gold ingots of Padre LaFarge.

More time passed, and one day Lopat spotted LaFarge, clothed in his priestly garb, strolling down a Santa Fe street. When Lopat greeted him, LaFarge told him that Indians had killed all of the other Frenchmen and that only he, LaFarge, knew the location of the treasure cache. He told Lopat that he was making arrangements for an expedition to return to the spring to retrieve the gold and wanted him to serve as guide.

Lopat immediately suspected LaFarge of killing the other Frenchmen and was convinced that once his service to the ex-priest was over that he too would be killed. LaFarge told Lopat that he would be richly compensated for his service as a guide, but the Spaniard said he wanted to think about the offer for a few days.

While Lopat was stalling for time before responding to LaFarge's invitation, the renegade priest was identified by two miners who had been members of a party that had been attacked months earlier by the priest and his gang and had their gold stolen. They enlisted several Santa Fe residents to their cause and before long a large mob roamed the streets of Santa Fe in search of LaFarge. The ex-priest hid beneath a load of furs that were being transported out of Santa Fe in a wagon but he was discovered and captured several miles east of the city. He was killed and buried in an unmarked grave.

With the death of LaFarge went the knowledge of the exact location of the treasure cache. Based on the scanty information provided him by the ex-priest, Lopat was convinced he could return to the spring and recover the treasure. He made the long journey but had no success in finding the buried ingots.

During the following decades, the story of the lost treasure of Padre LaFarge evolved into legend, one widely told. Though many were excited about the possibility of locating and recovering the immense treasure of five hundred gold ingots, there are no records of any attempts to do so until recently.

In 1870, however, a number of strange stone makings were discovered near the old Spanish Trail. The markers were fashioned from large rocks rolled into position to form the shape of a V. The point of each V was oriented in the direction of the next marker that was located anywhere from five to ten miles away. These odd directional markers were found to have been placed in a somewhat regular pattern from Santa Fe to the New Mexico settlement of Las Vegas, a distance of fifty-miles. Beyond Las Vegas, however, no more of the stone markers could be located.

Then, in 1876 and 1877, several more of the strange stone markers were found along the old road to Clayton, New Mexico, in the northeastern part of the state and just a few miles west of the western tip of the Oklahoma Panhandle. No one knew what to make of the markers.

In 1900, an area rancher named Ryan, along with some ranch hands, was driving a newly purchased herd of horses from Clayton to his ranch in Cimarron County. One evening as the cowboys were making camp, several of the horses broke away and scattered off onto the nearby plains. The next morning, Ryan and one of his cowhands went in search of them. Following several hours of tracking, the two men stopped to rest themselves and their mounts. As Ryan was scanning the countryside looking for his horses, he spotted a stone marker constructed of large rock and in the shape of a V.

Ryan, who was familiar with the legend of the lost gold of Padre LaFarge, was convinced that this series of stone markers pointed the way to the treasure. Over the next several years when Ryan found some spare time, he searched for more of the markers and found several. All of them led him to the general vicinity of Flagg Spring. Ryan searched the area around the spring for several years but never found the gold.

Ryan's nephew was a man named Cy Strong who had a ranch close to Sugar Loaf Mountain. Like Ryan, Strong was also convinced the treasure was buried close to the spring. Not far from Flagg Spring, Strong found the remains of an old dugout along with rock and remains of adobe that once comprised a dwelling. In addition, he found several pieces of rotted oxcart wheels. A few years later, however, Strong found more of the stone markers that he claimed suggested the treasure may have been buried closer to Sugar Loaf Mountain.

Since the discovery of the markers by Ryan and Strong, a number of search parties have arrived in the area of Flagg Spring to look for Padre LaFarge's buried gold ingots. To date, none have been successful.

If found today, LaFarge's cache would be worth untold millions. Professional treasure hunters who have employed low level aircraft flights accompanied by aerial photography, including infrared, insist that it is just a matter of time before the secret location of the gold ingots is revealed. The search continues.

Flat Top Mountain Treasure

Flat Top Mountain is an unremarkable landform located between the Quartz Mountains and Devil's Canyon in southwestern Oklahoma. Somewhere along the flanks of Flat Top Mountain a fortune in gold coins is buried. A small time outlaw named Bob Herring who died while serving a prison term cached the coins and was never able to return to the site to retrieve them.

Bob Herring was born in Eastland County, Texas, in 1870, about 170 straight-line miles southwest of Dallas. From the time he was a child, Herring had a passion for riding horses. So great was this infatuation and zeal that he would occasionally steal mounts from neighboring ranches, ride them for a few days, and then return them before anyone was the wiser.

Herring soon became adept at stealing horses, and before long he was accumulating and driving herds of a dozen or more from Texas into Indian Territory to sell to the tribes. It was during one of these trips that Herring met Joe Baker. Baker was well known in the Territories as a ruthless outlaw who would steal anything and resell it. If someone attempted to interfere with one of Baker's robberies, he was more often than not shot down.

In a short time, Herring and Baker became friends, and the latter invited the now twenty-four-year-old Herring to join his gang, consisting only of Baker and Herring, a man called Buck, and half-breed known only as Six Toes.

Several weeks later, the Baker gang rode up on a small party of cattlemen near Vernon, Texas. The men were returning from a livestock auction. Between them, the cattlemen had recently sold hundreds of head of livestock and were carrying a total of $35,000 in gold coins in their saddlebags. At gunpoint, Baker and his gang took the money and fled northward. Their intention was to reach the hill and mountain country of southwestern Oklahoma near Quartz Mountain and hide out.

Prior to crossing the Red River, Baker decided to locate a suitable place to set up camp for a few days to rest horses and men. Most of their rations had been depleted and Baker told Herring that since he was the newest member of the gang he had to go out and hunt for game for the evening meal.

During much of the ride from Vernon to the campsite, Baker, Buck, and Six Toes engaged in whispered conversations among themselves, and Herring began to suspect they were plotting something against him. After checking his rifle for loads, Herring mounted his horse and set out to search for game. Suspicious, he rode in a circle and approached the camp from the opposite direction. After dismounting and tying his horse to a tree two hundreds yards from the campsite, Herring, using caution, crept close enough to listen to the conversation of the gang members.

Herring arrived in time to hear Baker tell Buck and Six Toes that on his return, he was to be shot as he climbed down from his horse. Baker told the two men that the loot would then be split three ways instead of four. Buck and

Six Toes argued that trying to shoot Herring while he was carrying a rifle could backfire on them. They insisted that they wait until he had crawled into his bedroll for the night and kill him in his sleep. Baker agreed.

Herring returned to his mount. During the next hour he searched for game and was successful in bringing down two prairie chickens. When he returned to the camp, he cleaned the birds and handed them over to the others to cook. Herring noticed that the three men remained silent and furtive, giving him reason to stay alert as he went about unsaddling his horse and performing other chores.

The evening was warm and still as Baker positioned the birds on a spit over the fire to roast them. Seeking relief from the heat, all of the outlaws but Herring removed their shirts. Herring noted that Buck and Six Toes had set their pistols on their bedrolls before walking over to sit with Baker near the fire. Baker had a pistol tucked into his belt.

Herring laid his own rifle on his bedroll but kept his pistol in his holster, still belted around his waist. Watching the three outlaws engaged in conversation, Herring decided it would be a good time to make his move. He walked to position between them and their weapons. When the three men looked up, he pulled his pistol and aimed it at Baker. He then ordered the three stunned men to lie facedown on the ground.

He removed Baker's pistol and threw it into the nearby brush. Following this, he tied up each of the bandits. While Baker, Buck, and Six Toes hurled curses, Herring collected the remaining weapons and tossed them as far as he could. He then gathered the saddlebags filled with gold coins, some of the provisions, and loaded them onto his horse and two others. After chasing off the remaining horses, he mounted up and rode away, leading the packed horses along on a rope.

Herring rode in a northeasterly direction toward the Wichita Mountains all night long. The horses were tiring from the heavy loads of gold coins. As the sun was coming up, he stopped long enough to make coffee and allow the animals some rest.

Two days later, Herring arrived at Flat Top Mountain, located just to the west of Devil's Canyon. After searching the flanks of the mountains, he found a suitable location under a protruding rock. Beneath this rock Herring excavated a shallow hole into which he placed the saddlebags filled with gold coins. Before covering the cache with what he later described to a friend as a distinctive looking rock, Herring removed $4,000. He could live well on $4,000, he determined, until such time as he could return to this area and retrieve more of the gold coins. From Flat Top Mountain, Herring traveled to Kansas. Following a short time there, he went to Montana. After the passage of several more months, Herring decided to return to Texas.

At the first opportunity after freeing themselves of their bonds, Baker, Buck, and Six Toes located the loose horses and set out in search of Herring with the intention of retrieving the gold coins and killing him. Baker learned of Herring's trip to Montana and followed him there. While Baker was attempting to steal a fresh horse, however, he was shot and killed.

At one point, Six Toes learned that Herring was living in Austin, Texas, and went there in search of him. Shortly after arriving in town, Six Toes got into an argument with a citizen and murdered him. He was arrested, tried, and sentenced to a long term at the Texas State Prison in

Huntsville. During an escape attempt, he was shot and killed by a guard.

Months later while Herring was seated at a card table with several other gamblers, he spotted Buck eyeing him from the bar several feet away. At one point when Buck's attention was distracted, Herring left the table and dashed to his hotel room for his pistol. After entering the hotel, he looked behind him and saw that Buck was watching him from across the street.

Herring locked himself in his hotel room, anticipating that Buck would eventually come. It was not long in happening. During the early hours of the morning, Herring heard footsteps in the hall outside his room. Whoever was in the hallway was approaching with caution. Herring decided to surprise his visitor. In a single swift movement he opened the door to this room, leaned out into the hall, and fired several shots at the intruder. Buck was killed immediately, as were two innocent bystanders.

Several minutes later, law enforcement authorities arrived and arrested Herring. He was found guilty of murdering three people and sentenced to thirty-five years in the prison at Huntsville.

In 1920, a man named Josh Drake purchased a ranch not far from Mangum, Oklahoma, and about fifteen miles west of Flat Top Mountain. Drake was a cousin to Bob Herring, but he had no knowledge of the Flat Top Mountain treasure cache.

Drake made an annual journey to Texas to purchase cattle. During one of these trips, he stopped by the Hunstville State Prison to visit Herring. The prisoner told Drake that he had been the only person to pay him a visit during his time in prison. Drake continued to stop at the prison and spend a short time with Herring each year. During his 1930 visit, Drake was accompanied by his son, Josh, Jr. The boy was thirteen years old and fascinated with the prospect of meeting a relative who was a real life outlaw.

When the Drakes were admitted to the visiting room, they found Herring in poor health, wasted from tuberculosis. Herring was delighted to company and particularly enjoyed the young boy. He told Drake that, in gratitude, he would tell him the location of a buried fortune in gold coins.

During the next hour, Herring related the events that led to the burying of the gold at Flat Top Mountain. He provided directions as best as he could recall them, and even sketched a crude map. He said he covered the cache site with a "peculiar looking rock." Five months later, Drake received word that Herring had died.

Though intrigued with the prospect of finding a wealth of gold coins buried at Flat Top Mountain, Drake remained occupied with operating his ranch. In addition, Drake was not entirely convinced of the existence of the buried treasure, consigning much of the story to the ramblings of an old man.

Josh, Jr., however, had no doubt that Herring was telling the truth, and constantly pleaded with his father to find time for them to make a trip to the mountain to search for the treasure. Finally, the father consented.

Following Herring's description and map, they had no trouble locating Flat Top Mountain. In spite of spending a week searching for the cache, they had no success and were forced to return to the ranch.

Years passed, and Josh Drake, Jr. eventually left the ranch for college. When World War II broke out he joined the military and fought in the Pacific theater where he was wounded and eventually shipped home. For the rest of his life, Drake, Jr. searched for Bob Herring' lost cache of gold coins at Flat Top Mountain but could never find it.

The flanks of Flat Top Mountain provide an endless number of places to hide a treasure. And "peculiar looking rocks" can be found in abundance. There is little doubt among researchers that Bob Herring's cache of gold coins still resides in the place where it was initially buried well over a century ago. That it has not been found is likely due to the fact that this tale is not well known and few have attempted to search for the gold. Given the phenomenal increase in the value of gold since Herring buried it, the cache would be worth several million dollars if found today.

Outlaw Bill Cook's Lost Treasure Cache

During the 1880s and 1890s, a man named Bill Cook was a well-known outlaw who terrorized southern Oklahoma. Less famous than other Oklahoma-based outlaws such as Frank and Jesse James, the Dalton Gang, and the Youngers, Cook nevertheless was a successful bandit, making his living rustling cattle, robbing banks and trains, and preying on lone travelers. Short of temper and patience, Cook was known to shoot his victims if they manifested even the slightest resistance.

In October of 1894, Bill Cook and a rag-tag gang of ne'er-do-wells robbed a Rock Island Pacific train a few miles northeast of Ardmore. As the train pulled into a remote switching station to take on water, Cook and his five companions watched from hiding in a nearby copse of trees. During the water stop, the outlaws rode from their place of concealment and approached the train.

As the train was preparing to depart, one of the outlaws climbed into the engine cab and pulled his pistol on the engineer and fireman. At the same time, Cook and the rest of the gang entered the passenger cars and relieved travelers of their money, watches, and jewelry. This done, the outlaws broke into the mail car and blew open the safe. From this they removed $62,000 in gold and silver coins.

The coins were placed into gunnysacks which were, in turn, packed into their saddlebags. The outlaws then remounted and rode away toward the south.

As the outlaws headed for the Red River Valley, a mounted force of deputized lawmen was already in pursuit. At one point during their flight, the outlaws spotted the lawmen two miles behind them and gaining. Cook decided to try to lose the posse employing unorthodox measures. Turning toward the northeast, he led the gang along a zigzag course, eventually crossing the Little Blue River north of Tishomingo days later. They were now twenty-five miles northeast of the station where they committed the robbery.

The heavy loads of gold and silver coins were taking a toll on the tiring horses. At one point, Cook made the decision to stop and set up camp in a thicket on the west bank of Delaware Creek (now called Delaware River). Here, said Cook, they would divide the loot and ride out in different directions.

Following the evening meal, Cook carried the bags of gold and silver coins, jewelry, and watches to a point near the campfire. As Cook counted out the coins in the light of the fire, he noted that three members of his gang were positioning themselves around him, hands on their pistols. Realizing they were intent on killing him and taking the gold and silver for themselves, Cook drew his own handgun and shot the closest outlaw, killing him. Within seconds, the other two were dead. The two remaining outlaws ran for their horses, mounted up, and escaped into the night.

Fearing that the two men might return, Cook repacked all of the coins and other loot, loaded them onto his horse as well as three others that had belonged to his dead companions and rode away. In the moonlight, Cook made his way some distance from the previous camp. Behind him, he could hear the shouts of the pursuing lawmen as they discovered the dead bodies of the outlaws.

Realizing the weary horses were no longer capable of transporting the heavy loads, Cook decided to bury the loot. After dismounting, he scraped out a shallow hole, placed the coin- and jewelry-filled bags into it, and covered them over. Making note of what landmarks he could in the dark of night, he remounted and rode away.

Moments later, Cook heard the sounds of pursuit. Riding to the top of a nearby ridge, he spotted the posse only five hundred yards away and gaining fast. Guiding his horse down the opposite side of the ridge, he spurred the tired animal, coaxing it to greater speeds.

His efforts to escape came for naught. The posse men were now close enough to fire their weapons. One of their bullets struck Cook in the shoulder, nearly knocking him from the saddle. Eventually, weakened by loss of blood, he paused at the bank of a river preparatory to crossing and then fell from his horse, unconscious.

Unlikely as it seems, the posse, now only a few dozen yards behind Cook, failed to spot him lying on the riverbank. They found his horse, conducted a cursory search for the outlaw, and then rode away.

Early the next morning, an area resident named Charley Barnett arrived at the river. Barnett intended to spend the morning fishing. As he set out three cane poles and baited the hooks, he spotted Cook lying on the riverbank a short distance upstream. So much blood had leaked from the man onto the sand that Barnett thought he was dead. On investigating, however, Barnett discovered he was still breathing, but just barely. Barnett raced home, retrieved a wagon, and returned. After loading the man, he transported him to a doctor in the nearby tiny settlement of Tupelo.

When Cook regained his senses, he found himself lying in a bed in a strange room. Standing over him was the doctor. Seated nearby was Barnett. The two men explained to Cook the circumstances under which he was found and how he finally arrived at the doctor's home. The doctor told him he had lost a lot of blood and would likely have died had not Barnett found him and delivered him for treatment.

Finished with his ministrations for the time being, the doctor left the room. Cook asked Barnett to join him at his bedside, and when he did he told him of the train robbery, the $62,000, the watches and jewelry, the flight from the law, the killing of his fellow outlaws, the reburying of the loot, and his subsequent failure to escape.

Then, Cook surprised Barnett by telling him where the buried treasure was located, and said that he was giving it to him for saving his life. Cook provided Barnett with a detailed description of the location where the treasure was cached.

Three days later, Cook climbed out of his bed, dressed, and crept out of the doctor's house. More time passed, and the outlaw eventually made his way to New Mexico in search of ranch work on. He was recognized, arrested, and shipped to Fort Smith, Arkansas, where he found himself in the court of Judge Isaac Parker. Found guilty of twelve counts of robbery, Cook was sentenced to forty-five years in the federal prison in Albany, New York. He died in prison before his time was served.

For years, Barnett' resisted the temptation to travel to the location described by Cook in an attempt to retrieve the treasure in gold and silver coins and jewelry. He feared that the surviving outlaws involved in the train robbery were also searching for it and did not want to chance an encounter. Time passed. When Barnett learned that Cook was in prison, he related to a federal marshal what Cook had told him about the buried loot. The marshal conducted a search for the cache but never found it.

Years later, Barnett was interviewed by amateur lost treasure historian Maurice Kildare and told him, as near as he could remember, the directions to the cache as provided by Cook. He stated that the treasure was buried on "this side of Delaware Creek and could be as far away as Dunk McMillan's pasture on the edge of the prairie. Start your hunt on a line between the creek and where I found the manganese."

The manganese referred to by Barnett consisted of large black rocks, some of which were almost six feet tall. According to the descriptions Barnett provided Kildare, the trail from the field of manganese ran toward the Delaware River then turned eastward. He insisted that this detail was considered by Cook to be important.

Kildare, in the company of five other men (but apparently without Barnett), went in search of the Cook's buried treasure cache. Off and on for several months, the men looked for the treasure but had no success. During one of their trips into the field, they were convinced they found outlaw Cook's last campsite. They discovered three skeletons that they were certain belonged to the train robbers killed by Cook.

Following the most likely trail Cook would have taken from this campsite, the searchers arrived at a property once owned by a man named McMillan and later sold to a farmer named Dotson. They concentrated their energies here, but years of heavy rains, flash floods, and wildfires had altered the environment so that it bore little resemblance to the descriptions provided by Cook.

The old Dotson field has long since grown over. As far as is known, no one employing a metal detector has ever conducted a search of the area for Cook's buried loot. Cook himself stated that the gold and silver coins were buried in a shallow excavation, and it is suspected that today they lie only a few inches below the surface.

The likelihood of finding outlaw Cook's buried treasure is good. If recovered today, the $62,000 value of the coins in 1894 would be worth many times that amount.

Lost Gold Coin Cache in Sequoyah County

A Cherokee Indian named Usray lived with his son, daughter-in-law, and grandson in a small log cabin in the wooded foothills of Oklahoma's Ozark Mountains a short distance east of the present-day town of Sallisaw. Usray had been granted a parcel of land on which he raised a few crops along with chickens, hogs, and a few cattle. Usray was best known, however, as a breeder of fine horses. Anyone living in the area who had need of a good work animal, a decent riding horse, or even a blooded racing horse would visit the Usray farm.

As the Civil War got under way, soldiers from both the Union and Confederate armies occupied parts of Indian Territory. While no major battles were fought in the region, various aspects of the war inflicted elements of tragedy on many of the region's residents. The Indians who lived in the area were, for the most part, neutral during the conflict—they held no allegiances to either side and had no interest in the philosophical differences between northern and southern white men.

When northern soldiers moved into Indian Territory and occupied the region, they occasionally found it necessary to replenish their supply of riding stock. They soon learned that the best horseflesh to be obtained in the Ozarks belonged to Usray and could be purchased at reasonable prices. On several occasions they visited the Indian's farm to buy mounts and pack animals. With each transaction, a payment was made in gold coins. A frugal man who rarely left his farm, Usray had little need for money and worldly goods. Every time he was paid, he deposited his gold coins in a tin box that he kept hidden under the floor of cabin. He intended someday to give all of the money to his son.

As the War wound down, the Union soldiers gradually pulled out. Initially, Usray regretted the departure of the troopers and the loss of opportunity to conduct business with them. In addition, several of them had become friends and he knew he would miss them. With the soldiers gone, Usray felt that life in the Oklahoma Ozarks could get back to normal. He did not consider the fact that once the protection of the military was gone, outlaws would move into the area to prey on residents.

Concerned that his farm might be visited by bandits, Usray pastured his best stock in a hidden meadow several hundred yards from the cabin, hoping the animals would escape the notice of roving horse thieves.

Usray was also worried about the safety of the cache of gold hidden beneath the floor of his cabin. He removed the tin box filled with coins and added his wife's jewelry and a gold watch he had owned for years. He wrapped the box in an old sheepskin rug and told his grandson he was going to bury it in the woods where it would be safe from bandits. He invited the boy to go along.

The youngster walked with Usray as far as the spring from which the family drew water. Telling the boy to wait there, the old Indian slipped into the nearby hills. In one-half hour, he returned to the spring and told his grandson that he had buried the box where no one would ever find it.

That evening as the family sat down to dinner, they heard the approach of riders. Stopping in front of the cabin, the newcomers called out. Fearing that the men might be outlaws, Usray told his family to hide under the floor of the cabin. Then he stepped outside to greet the visitors.

Just beyond the small front porch four men sat on horseback. They were a scruffy lot and had the look of men used to hard living. The leader, who had a scarred face and long hair spilling out from under a wide-brimmed hat, spurred his horse a few steps closer. He wore several pistols in his belt and carried a rifle across his saddle. He told Usray that he was aware of a recent purchase made with gold coins and demanded that the money be turned over to him immediately.

With calm demeanor, Usray told the outlaw that he had earned the money and needed it for his family. He stated he was not about to turn it over to worthless men too lazy to work for a living.

Angered by the remark, the outlaw leader asked for the money again, telling the Indian that if he did not relinquish it he would pay with his life. In response, Usray folded his arms across his chest in a gesture of defiance and met the outlaw's hard gaze with his own.

The leader decided to employ an oft-used tactic to convince Usray to part with his fortune. At a signal from him, one of the gang members tossed a rope over the Indian and pulled him off of the porch and into the dirt. Tying the other end of the rope around his saddle horn, the outlaw dragged Usray across the clearing to the edge of the woods near the spring. There, the bandits pulled the old man to his feet and demanded the gold coins once again. And again, the old man refused.

The end of the rope was untied from the saddle horn and thrown over the low-hanging limb of a nearby tree. A noose was fashioned and placed around Usray's neck. The outlaws pulled the Indian off the ground and let him hang for several seconds before allowing his to drop to the ground. Usray, coughing and choking, forced air into his lungs. At this point, his young grandson had crawled from his hiding place from under the cabin and watched in horror as the outlaws tortured his grandfather.

Several more times Usray was hoisted off the ground, the noose tightening and constricting his throat. Just when it seemed he was about to strangle, the outlaws would drop him to the ground and repeat their demand for the gold coins. Usray continued to refuse.

One of the outlaws removed Usray's moccasins and threatened to pull out his toenails. In response, the Indian spit in his face. As they removed the toenails, the old man did not give them the satisfaction of crying out in pain. Frustrated, the leader stabbed Usray in the heart and ordered his companions to hang the body from the limb.

The outlaws turned their attention to the cabin. They ransacked the small home until they were certain the gold was not there. Discouraged at finding nothing, they mounted up and rode away.

When the outlaws were gone the grandson informed the others and they came out from hiding. The boy told his parents what he had witnessed. They went to the spring, cut down the old man, and buried him.

The following morning, the boy told his parents about Usray hiding the tin box filled with gold coins and jewelry. Several attempts were made to locate the cache but it was never found.

When the boy grew to be a man, he returned to the area several times to search for his grandfather's cache, always entering the foothills from a point near the spring. He located a well-worn trail believed to be the one traveled by his grandfather, but was his search for the gold was unsuccessful.

Spanish Treasure in Tulsa

Sometime during the late eighteenth century, a party of sixteen Spaniards made its way across northeastern Oklahoma near the present-day city of Tulsa. In addition to several horses and burros laden with supplies and provisions, the Spaniards herded along twelve stout mules, each of them transporting gold ingots stuffed into leather bags that in turn were secured to wooden packsaddles.

Researchers are convinced that the gold came from a successful mining operation located somewhere in the Rocky Mountains, probably in Colorado. As with previous Spanish pack trains, researchers are also certain they were bound for a location on the Mississippi River where the gold would be loaded onto rafts and floated down to New Orleans. There, the ingots would be transferred onto awaiting ships and carried either to Mexico or across the Atlantic Ocean to Spain.

The Spaniards observed that they were being followed by a band of Indians. With each passing day, the Indians drew closer to the pack train. The Spaniards' route paralleled the Arkansas River. When the party arrived at a familiar crossing, they decided to stop and set up camp for the night. At this location was a fresh water spring, one often used by the Spaniards on previous expeditions. The spring was nine-feet in diameter and three feet deep. From one lip of the pond, a thin stream of water flowed out toward the nearby Arkansas River. The horses, mules, and burros were unpacked, fed, and staked out and cook fires started. Sentries were posted at the perimeter of the camp to guard against the potential threat of Indian attack.

Following the evening meal, the leader of the Spaniards assembled all of the men and explained that, since the Indians that had been trailing them were only a few hundreds yards behind, he anticipated they would attack on the morrow. To ensure the attackers would not come into possession of the gold, he explained that they would bury it nearby. Without the heavy gold to slow them, he felt certain they would escape and return with reinforcements at a later date and retrieve the ingots.

With that, the leader strode several paces from the spring and selected a site. Here, a deep hole was excavated and the gold-filled packs were placed within. The hole was then refilled and covered over to look much like the surrounding environment. This done, the shovels, along with other tools and gear, were tossed into the spring. The less equipment and gear they were forced to carry, explained the leader, the greater their chances for escape.

The following morning after a quick breakfast, the Spaniards mounted up and, leading the horses and mules, crossed the river and continued their journey eastward. For reasons that have never been explained, they never returned to the region to retrieve the gold.

With the passage of time, the town of Tulsa was established at this site. In 1828, it took form as a Creek Indian settlement called Talise, pronounced Tah-lee-Say. The whites living nearby referred to it as Tulsey Town. The Creeks were brought to this location from their homes in

Alabama and Georgia during the infamous Trail of Tears, a government-inflicted relocation program encouraged by white men who coveted the Indian lands of the southeastern United States. In time, the town was simply referred to as Tulsa.

In 1904, a stranger arrived in Tulsa, introduced himself as Fraley. He carried an old and well-worn map purporting to show the location of the gold ingots buried by the Spaniards over a century earlier. The map was eighteen-by-eighteen inches and, according to Fraley, was given to him by his father who claimed he obtained it from the descendant of a Spaniard whose ancestor was a member of the party that buried the gold.

According to the map, the gold ingots were buried several paces from a prominent spring located near a well-used ford on the Arkansas River. Close to the cache was a large cottonwood tree that bore markings made by the Spaniards that would help identify the location of the buried gold.

Not familiar with the area, Fraley enlisted the assistance of a local resident, a Creek Indian named William S. Foresman. Foresman had lived his entire life in Tulsa. In 1904, the town boasted a population of around 1,000 residents. One year later, the eastern Oklahoma oil boom would arrive and the town would grow exponentially.

Following the directions indicated on the map, Fraley and Foresman found themselves walking along the banks of the Arkansas River in the area of Tulsa's Twenty-first Street. At one point, Foresman pointed to a location on the river he called Gano's Crossing. The crossing was named after a Confederate army officer, Brigadier General Richard M. Gano during the Civil War. Gano, along with the famous Cherokee leader Stand Watie, led a Confederate raid that employed the ford to cross over one hundred wagons captured from Union forces at what has been called the Second Battle of Cabin Creek. Prior to Gano's use of the ford, it was a crossing often used by the various Indian tribes that lived in and/or frequented the area. It was one of the few places along the river that was underlain by a limestone outcrop that provided for a solid bottom.

Near Gano's Crossing, they encountered a small stream that entered the larger river and turned to follow it to its source. Not far away, they came to a spring that matched the description of the one indicated on the map.

There were several cottonwood trees in the area, and following nearly an hour of searching, the two men found one that manifested a patch of healed over bark four-feet above the ground. After peeling away the bark, they found the markings alluded to on the map. The markings include several signs and numbers, along with a few words in Spanish. None of it, however, could be deciphered by Fraley or Foresman.

Using four-feet long thin metal rods, Fraley and Foresman probed the soil in and around the spring but found nothing. A few days later, Fraley and Foresman learned of a Tulsa resident who claimed to be able to dowse for gold and other precious metals. After he was brought to the spring, the dowser employed a divining rod that he felt certain would show them the location of the gold. Repeatedly, the divining rod pointed toward the center of the spring.

Over the next few days, Fraley and Foresman dug a ditch to drain the water from the spring. This done, they dug into the soft mud and silt of the bottom, convinced that every shovelful of the muck they removed would bring them closer to the fortune in gold ingots.

After excavating down two feet, Fraley's shovel struck something that yielded the sound of metal. Imbued with excitement, the men redoubled their efforts and, moments later, pulled from the mud an ancient shovel blade with a partially rotted handle. Boosted by their discovery, they returned with the dowser once again and requested a new reading. And once more, the dowser's divining rod pointed downward toward the center of the spring.

Fraley and Foresman continued shoveling. After each shovelful of mud and silt was removed, the viscous muck slowly refilled the excavation. They redoubled their efforts, and after two more hours of digging, another shovel blade was found. Once again the dowser was summoned, but his divining rod failed to pick up a signal.

Fraley and Foresman dug a few holes near the spring but failed to locate anything of value. After two weeks in Tulsa, Fraleys' funds were exhausted. Disappointed, he returned to wherever he had come. As far as is known, he never attempted to locate the cache of coins again.

On January 1, 1933, the story of the Spanish gold cache and Fraley's attempts to locate it appeared in an issue of the *Tulsa Daily World.* The article, titled "Legend Says Gold Lies Beneath Tulsa Soil," generated a number of searches for the cache, all ending in failure.

By 1933, the spring had been filled in. The location was one block south of the Eleventh Street bridge and just east of Riverside Drive and just north of Gano's Crossing (sometimes referred to as Gano's Ford on maps). Today this entire region is covered with houses, and the old stream that once led from the spring to the river is now a storm drain.

It has been suggested by some that the buried cache of Spanish gold ingots, estimated to be worth millions of dollars, may very well lie buried in the yard of a Tulsa resident. It has also been proposed that a state-of-the-art metal detector might be successful in locating it.

Outlaw Coin Cache

According to the physician in charge, the man lying on the hospital cot was dying and would likely not live more than another day or two. He had suffered numerous wounds that had been cleaned and bandaged. In the process, the doctor removed seven bullets and three arrowheads. Many of the wounds were near vital organs and a great deal of blood had been lost.

The patient was only vaguely aware of others in the hospital room. He had been semi-conscious and in great pain when he had been carried in and sedated with morphine. At one point a nurse bent over him to wipe his fevered head with a cool rag. He perceived her soothing words and tried to communicate with her. Through the haze of sedation he managed to croak out the words "the money," "buried," and "friends dead." His throat was parched and his lips dry and cracked, and the words came out as raspy and cryptic utterances that the nurse was not certain she understood.

In spite of the doctor's prediction that the patient would soon die, he roamed in and out of consciousness on his hospital cot for the next two weeks. On several occasions he tried to talk, but the results were always the same. At one point, he made a feeble attempt to reach out to the nurse, but the effort caused him to drop into unconsciousness once again.

The patient, estimated to be around thirty-five years of age, continued in this condition for days, getting no better. He possessed no identification and no one in the hospital or the city of Dallas had ever seen him before. From time to time it appeared as though he was experiencing bad dreams as he would cry out and thrash about on his cot. When this happened, the nurse would sit with him and try to calm him. She reported that the man had been crying, large tears coursing down his cheeks.

One day as the nurse was spoon-fed some broth into the patient's mouth, he opened his eyes and rose up on the cot. He looked around, confused. As she assisted him in lying back down, the patient gently took hold of her hand and asked her to sit with him for a while.

For an hour the nurse remained, neither of them speaking. Finally, the patient looked up at the nurse, told her his name was John, and asked her permission to allow him to explain to her the events that had led to his arrival at the hospital and how he had acquired his wounds. She acquiesced. As the nurse listened, the dying man, in halting speech, unfolded an incredible tale of a bank robbery, a harrowing escape across the Oklahoma prairie, a deadly fight with Indians, the deaths of his two companions, and the hasty burial of a fortune in gold and silver coins.

Two months earlier, the man who lay dying on the hospital cot had experienced, along with his two companions, a disappointing season on the buffalo range. For several years John and his partners, whom he referred to as Kelly and Morton, had made their living as hide hunters. That year, however, the herds had dwindled and were in danger of being hunted out. The men often talked of finding some other line of work, but grudgingly admitted none of them knew how to do anything but shoot and skin buffalo.

On a cool evening while seated around a campfire somewhere in western Kansas, one of the hide hunters suggested they rob a bank. Following further discussion of their bad luck in the hide business and acknowledging they possessed only five dollars between them and had no chance of finding work, the notion of robbing a bank began to sound promising.

Several days later the three men arrived in Wichita, at the time a bustling community. They set up camp outside of town and invested three days observing the comings and goings at one of the banks. Convinced they could pull off their plan, they decided to rob the bank when it opened the next morning.

The owner of the bank was unlocking the front door at precisely 9:00 a.m. when John approached him from behind, shoved the barrel of his revolver into the small of his back, and ordered him inside. Kelly followed while Morton stood guard outside. Within minutes, several canvas bags were filled with gold and silver coins from the bank's vault. The banker was tied, gagged, and placed on the floor behind his own desk. Carrying the heavy sacks, the three bank robbers exited the bank. They strapped the sacks onto their horses, mounted up, and rode out of town.

For the next two days, John, Kelly, and Morton traveled in a southerly direction. They rode their horses hard, stopping only long enough to allow them to water and graze. The three men subsisted on biscuits they had made in camp several days earlier. On the third day the horses, unaccustomed to the combined heavy weight of riders and coins, began to falter and stumble.

On that afternoon, the three bank robbers crossed the line into Indian Territory. In desperate need of rest, they pulled into a grove of elm trees near the trail and set up camp. Around the campfire that night, they counted the money they had taken from the bank. They were surprised to discover it totaled nearly $50,000. They decided to continue on to Texas and use the money to purchase a ranch.

For the next few days, the bank robbers continued on an erratic southerly course toward Texas. One afternoon while riding across open prairie, Morton's horse went lame, forcing them to a halt. After examining the mount, Morton declared the animal would not last much longer. He was concerned that he would have to walk. John and Kelly were worried that their horses were not up to the task of transporting the extra load. They proceeded southward, more slowly, constantly stopping to rest the tired horses.

As the three men passed through a portion of present-day Caddo County southwest of Oklahoma City, Kelly, who was familiar with the area, informed his companions that they were not far from the Wichita Mountains. There, he said, they would find fresh water, shelter, and an abundance of wild game. It would be an ideal place to rest after the long and tiring journey.

The respite in the Wichita Mountains was not as peaceful as they hoped. From the day they entered the range, the three men spotted Indians watching them from the nearby hills. Kelley recognized them as Comanches and told his companions that they were regarded as the most bloodthirsty Indians to roam the Great Plains. Camp that evening was subdued and quiet, and none of the men got much sleep.

After three days in the mountain range, the outlaws packed up and continued on their journey. Though Morton's lame horse struggled with the heavy load, it was able to proceed at a cautious pace.

Later that same afternoon, the men stopped at a spring. As the horses watered and the outlaws munched on biscuits, Morton spotted forty mounted Comanches back on the trail they had just traveled. The Indians were heading toward the spring at a rapid pace. The outlaws mounted with haste and coaxed their weary horses southward. Moments later, the Comanches came in saw them. Voicing screams, the Indians, brandishing bows and arrows, lances, and rifles, pushed their horses to a gallop in pursuit.

After fleeing only a few hundred yards, it became clear to the outlaws that their heavily laden mounts, along with the lame horse, could never outdistance the swift, plains-bred steeds of the Comanches. During their flight, Morton suggested to his companions that they cut loose the heavy sacks of coins to lighten their load. John and Kelley rejected the idea.

Of a sudden, Morton's horse stopped in its tracks, unable to go farther. It collapsed to the ground, throwing Morton and the money sacks to the side. John and Kelley turned their horses, dismounted, and, alongside Morton, took shelter behind the fallen animal. The lame horse kicked, thrashed, and tried to rise, so Kelley shot it through the head.

The Comanches reined up about one hundred yards away. From this position, they began lobbing arrows and firing bullets at three men hunkered behind the dead horse. For nearly an hour the Indians kept up the fusillade, keeping the three white men cowering behind the animal.

Morton, believing that a demonstration of bravery and firepower would discourage the attackers, rose up and took aim at a cluster of Indians on horseback. A second later, a bullet tore into his abdomen, and Morton dropped to the ground, writhing in pain.

For several hours, the Comanches continued firing away at the men behind the dead horse. Most of their bullets struck the dead horse and splattered blood onto the outlaws. Over one hundred arrows protruded from the horse's hide. Some of the Comanches positioned themselves to the side of the defensive position maintained by Kelly and John, but the skilled riflemen, experienced from so many buffalo hunts, kept them at a distance.

At sunset, Morton died from his wound. As John and Kelly sat in terrified silence against the dead horse, the Comanches retreated one-half mile back up the trail where they set up camp for the night.

When it grew dark, John and Kelly spotted the Indians' campfire in the distance. They presumed the Comanches had abandoned the siege for the night. Using their belt knives, the two men scraped out a shallow hole and buried Morton.

The two survivors sat in the dark considering their options. Kelley suggested they make a run for it. While John maintained a lookout for the Indians in the distance, Kelley went in search of their horses and found them grazing a quarter of a mile away, still saddled and still carrying the sacks of stolen gold and silver coins.

When Kelley returned with the horses, the two men retrieved Morton's share of the bank robbery loot and distributed it between the two mounts. Once the horses were loaded, the men mounted up and slipped away toward the south. Just as they abandoned the defensive position afforded by Morton's dead horse, a hint of dawn appeared on the eastern horizon and began illuminating the stark prairie. They had covered little more than a mile when they heard the screams of the Comanches in pursuit. Spurring their horses, each one now encumbered with far more weight than before, the outlaws tried to coax the animals to greater speeds.

With the Comanches almost upon them Kelley spotted a buffalo wallow, a shallow depression in the prairie, and guided his horse toward it. John followed. With little protection, the two men hunkered down and fired into the attacking line of Indians, killing several. During the next hour, both John and Kelley received wounds from Comanche bullets and arrows.

For the rest of the day, the Indians launched frontal attacks only to be repelled by the bullets from the large buffalo rifles. Around noon, Kelley was killed when a bullet slammed into this face. John, having lost a great deal of blood from his wounds, was able to maintain his defensive position until sundown. The Comanches once again rode off some distance away and set up camp.

For the second night in a row, John buried a friend. Into the shallow hole he scraped out in the bottom of the buffalo wallow, he placed Kelley's body, his saddle, two pistols, and his rifle. After covering the grave with dirt, John spotted the two horses grazing nearby. He retrieved them and led them to a nearby rise in the prairie where a lone tree grew. Here, he untied the sacks of coins from the horses. Weakened by loss of blood, John nevertheless excavated a second hole into which he placed the robbery loot. He unsaddled one of the horses and turned it loose. Mounting the other, he continued on toward Texas.

After riding away from the only tree that could be seen on that section of prairie, John crossed what he identified as West Cache Creek, a landmark he intended to use when he returned to retrieve the treasure. Days later, John forded the Red River and entered Texas. He finally arrived in Dallas before dawn one day. His ordeal, along with the long journey, had weakened John to a point close to death. At sunrise, he was found lying in the middle of the town's main street, his horse standing over him. His fall from the horse had reopened his wounds and a great deal of blood had leaked from his body to pool in the street. He was carried to the hospital.

When John finished relating his tale to the nurse, he breathed a deep sigh and stated that he believed he was going to die and that he would never be able to return to Indian Territory to retrieve the buried fortune in gold and silver coins. John asked the nurse to locate it for him and return it to the bank in Wichita, Kansas. He provided her with directions to the lone tree on the prairie and sketched a crude map. Two days later, John died in his sleep.

The nurse did not act immediately on John's request and told no one else about the cache of money. Several years later, she resigned her position at the hospital, organized a small expedition, and set out for Indian Territory in an attempt to locate John's buried treasure.

Following the directions she was provided, she concentrated her search in an area four miles west-southwest of the present-day town of Geronimo near the boundary that separates Comanche and Cotton Counties. The landscape she encountered here matched the descriptions provided by John. Her search for the treasure was hampered, however, by the continued presence of

Indians who harassed the party from the moment it arrived. Discouraged, the nurse abandoned the search and returned to Dallas. She never made another attempt to retrieve the outlaw's treasure cache.

For many years, only a handful of people were aware of the story of the buried cache of gold and silver coins. The few that did were apprised of the story as a result of an article that appeared in the October 18, 1907 issue of the Lawton, Oklahoma, *Daily News-Republican*. Under the headline "Human Form Unearthed in Big Pasture," the article related how two Cotton County farmers found the muzzle of a rifle sticking out of the ground and decided to investigate. After digging a few inches into the soil, they found, in addition to the rifle, a complete human skeleton, two pistols, and a saddle. The saddle was described as being in fairly good condition. When it was cleaned up, the name A.E. Kelley was found branded onto the skirts.

To those who were aware of the significance of this find, it meant that the treasure was buried nearby on a low rise in the prairie atop which grew a solitary tree. Unfortunately for hopeful treasure hunters, the two farmers refused to reveal the location of their find, stating only that it was in an old buffalo wallow not far from West Cache Creek.

In 1910, another important discovery was made. Less than three miles north of where Kelley's remains were found, a second human skeleton was discovered when runoff from a severe rainstorm eroded a shallow incision into the surface of the prairie. This skeleton, found alongside another of a horse, and was in the exact location the nurse believed the three outlaws initially defended themselves against the attacking Comanches. The remains were undoubtedly those of Morton.

To date, there is no evidence that the $50,000 in gold and silver coins (in late nineteenth century values) buried on the Oklahoma plains near West Cache Creek has ever been found.

Creek Indian Settlement Treasure

A short time after the onset of the Civil War, the United States Government made a hefty payment to a band of Creek Indians that had been relocated to Indian Territory. The money, believed to have been $100,000 in twenty-dollar gold pieces, was an annuity payment made according to the terms of an earlier treaty. The money was to be distributed among the members of the tribe. Logistical difficulties made immediate payments impossible, and as a result the gold coins were buried, a measure taken by the chief until such time as the others could be located, informed, and organized. As a result of compelling circumstances, none of this happened, and the fortune in gold coins still lies cached in a shallow hole in McIntosh County, Oklahoma.

The chief of the Creeks during this time was a man named Hopoithle Yoloho (also spelled Opthle Yahola in some records). After being removed from parts of Alabama and resettled in Indian Territory, Yoloho and his people adapted readily, built a small community, and established productive farms at a location called Brush Hill.

At the time Yoloho received the payment, the greatest majority of his band had scattered into remote areas in the nearby hills in response to growing fear of war in the region. The Creek Indians had had enough of the white man's dominance, aggression, and dishonesty. They wished to be as far way from them as possible.

While waiting for his people to reunite, Yoloho hid the gold coins. With the help of a fellow tribesman, the money was placed in a large wooden trunk. Too heavy for the two men to lift, Yoloho enlisted the services of four black men to assist in transporting it to a preselected location. Not far from Brush Hill, an excavation was made, the trunk filled with the coins placed within, and the hole covered over. Nearby, noted Yaholo, was a large oak tree. To insure the secrecy of the location, Yoloho then killed the four helpers.

In time, members of the Creek tribe drifted back to the settlement, but before the payment could be dug up and distributed, the threat of roving bands of both Union and Confederate soldiers, as well as bandits, arose again. This time, Yoloho gathered his people and set out for a location in Kansas where they were guaranteed protection by Union forces. Before leaving, Yoloho explained to them that, on their return, the government payment would be recovered and distributed among them.

This did not happen. The tribe set out for Kansas, most of them on foot and carrying only what they deemed necessary. A few days after leaving their land in McIntosh County, they were attacked by Confederate guerillas. Unprepared for such an event and poorly armed, many were killed. The survivors fled into the woods. Among those killed during the first wave of the attack was Yoloho's friend who had helped him bury the gold coins. Yoloho himself was wounded.

Later, the ragged band of Creeks crossed the border into Kansas. Before another day passed, Yoloho died. Before the chief succumbed, he told a fellow tribesman named Joe

Grayson that the gold coins had been buried near a fork in the road a short distance north of Brush Hill and not far from a large oak tree. Months later, Grayson traveled to the area but had no luck in locating the precise spot where the trunk was buried.

Today, as a result of increased population growth in this area, it is difficult to determine which forked road Yoloho was referring to before he died. There exist, however, pre-Civil War maps of the region that likely indicate the principal transportation and travel routes in the area of the Creek settlement known as Brush Hill.

Harmony Gold Coin Cache

John C. White owned and operated a small ranch a short distance from the tiny community of Harmony in Atoka County in southeastern Oklahoma. Today, Harmony is only known to some old-timers and few others, but during the early part of the twentieth century it was a service center for area ranchers and farmers.

White, a frugal man, earned money from the sale of his cattle and cotton crop during a period ranging from 1900 to 1923. He always requested that he be paid in gold coins. Distrustful of banks, as many were in those days, White preferred to stash his money close by where he could keep an eye on it. He placed his coins in fruit jars that he buried in a secret location near his house. He never revealed the location of the cache to his wife.

In 1923, White decided to travel to Texas to visit relatives. He left his wife at home on the ranch and told her he would return soon. White had grown elderly and was experiencing a difficult time keeping up with the obligations of running a ranch and cotton farm. He pondered the possibility of selling out and moving in with kin. Before leaving, he asked a neighbor, W.F. McKown, to mind his place for him. McKown agreed to do so. White also told McKown about his buried fortune in gold coins and stated his concern about strangers going onto his property and locating them. He explained that he had buried the coins near his house but he did not tell McKown where. White told McKown that he would not be gone long.

According to an interview with McKown several years later, White was concerned about the possibility of robbery and did not want to travel with his money. Despite McKown's suggestion that he deposit the money a bank to keep it safe, White refused.

A year passed and White had not returned to his ranch. A short time later, McKown received a letter from the old man. According to McKown, the letter contained an expression of gratitude for taking care of White's place. White also stated that he planned on returning and digging up his fortune as soon as he recovered from some unknown ailment. There was no explanation relative to what it was.

McKown continued to maintain White's ranch and look in on Mrs. White, but the old man never returned. Months later, McKown received a letter from White's relatives stating that he had passed away in Texas.

Though tempted, McKown stated that he never searched for White's gold. In conversations with White's widow, he learned that she was aware of the fortune in buried gold coins but had no inkling of their location.

Mrs. White continued to live on the ranch long after her husband's passing. She got along comfortably leasing the pastures and cotton fields to neighbors, one of whom was McKown.

In 1960, a couple arrived at McKown's ranch and expressed a desire to speak with him about John White's fortune in gold coins. They identified themselves as a nephew and niece of "Uncle John" and wanted to search for the gold that they claimed he told them was buried on his property. By this time, rancher McKown himself was no longer living, but they spent time visiting with his widow. According to Mrs. McKown, the young couple invested many hours digging around the old White house, but never found anything.

The location of the White ranch property is a matter of record at the Atoka County courthouse. Once this geography is established, a visit to the location should reveal the site of the ranch house. With the assistance of a good metal detector and permission from the property owner, it is entirely possible that the location of rancher White' buried wealth of gold coins could be determined.

Joseph Payne's Lost Vein of Silver

During the last half of the nineteenth century, the Ozark Mountain portion of what was then known as Indian Territory was sparsely settled. As a result, it became a desirable destination for outlaws and renegades, for few interfered with them and their activities. For decades, effective law enforcement ended at the western border of Arkansas and the outlaw element became relatively safe from pursuit. Some have estimated that the population of outlaws was greater than that of honest, law-abiding settlers.

From time to time, bands of outlaws ranged from their hideouts to conduct raids on farms, small towns, and travelers in neighboring Arkansas and Missouri. Murders, robberies, rapes, and other violent crimes were commonplace. When the outlaws completed their raiding, they retreated to the sanctuary of the forested and canyoned Ozark hills of Indian Territory.

These problems grew so serious that federal marshals were eventually ordered into remote parts of the Territory to capture the outlaws and return them to stand trial in Fort Smith, Arkansas, a court presided over by "Hanging Judge" Isaac Parker. Dozens of U.S. marshals and deputies operated throughout much of the eastern part of the Territory until Oklahoma achieved statehood in 1917.

Despite the wild, even primitive, and lawless conditions under which these men were forced to work, along with the inherent dangers associated with their task, they compiled an impressive record.

Among the most successful of these federal lawmen was Deputy United States marshal Joseph Payne. Payne was assigned to Judge Parker, who in turn sent him to patrol the wild and dangerous Ozark region of Indian Territory. During his first few months, Payne gained a reputation as a competent and effective lawman. Because of his successes, Parker gave him the most difficult assignments.

During the spring of 1881, Payne was ordered into the Ozark hills a few miles south of Tahlequah, some twenty miles west of the Arkansas line. The group of outlaws he was sent after numbered five. It was a testimony to Parker's confidence in Payne that he sent him out alone.

Payne tracked the outlaws for several days through the hills of this western fringe of the Ozarks until the trail led him to a narrow valley sheltered by steep bluffs. Leery of an ambush, Payne decided not to enter the area alone and decided to return to Fort Smith for reinforcements.

During the several days he spent tracking, Payne had exhausted most of his rations. As the area through which he was traveling manifested an abundance of wild game, he decided to do some hunting and smoke some meat. After staking out his horse in a narrow meadow, Payne took his rifle and followed fresh deer tracks into a promising looking stand of trees. The valley had been carved out by a small but fast-flowing stream that confluences with the Illinois River one mile to the west. Payne spotted several deer but none presented a clear shot. After hunting for two hours and having nothing to show for his effort, he paused by the stream to rest.

Payne removed one of his boots to check for wear on the sole when a glint of color from the stream, only a few inches deep, attracted his attention. Replacing the boot, he drew closer to the shallow creek and spotted a vein of color three feet wide and bisecting the limestone rock of the streambed. The vein disappeared under the stream bank on either side.

Payne stepped into the creek, and using his knife probed at the vein. The texture was soft, and he managed to pry out several small pieces. Returning to the bank, he examined his find and was surprised to discover it was almost pure silver. He returned to the creek, dug into the banks on both sides, and found that the vein continued for several yards in each direction.

The apparent high quality of the ore, the thickness of the vein, and the fact that it appeared to extend deep below the shallow layer of soil gave Payne reason to believe he had discovered a rich lode of silver.

Payne abandoned his hunt for deer and returned to Fort Smith as fast as possible. He requested and received leave from his duties as deputy marshal and returned to his discovery. On this trip, Payne carried along a hand drill that he used to test the depth of the vein. The drill was four feet long and he found silver at that depth just as pure as that which he dug from the surface. Payne estimated that he had several tons of rich ore just under his feet.

Payne was only too aware of the federal restrictions relative to prospecting and mining ore on Indian lands, so he decided to proceed with caution. In Fort Smith, he made discreet inquiries about the possibility of obtaining permission to mine in Indian Territory, but he was discouraged at every turn. He knew it would not be possible to conduct any kind of large-scale mining without being detected and he was unwilling to risk the penalties to which he would be subjected should he be discovered. During the next several months when he could find the time, Payne traveled to his secret location and dug out enough silver to fill a saddlebag with each visit. He never carried much of the ore at any one time for fear of arousing suspicion.

Payne's law enforcement duties often took him far from his silver, and sometimes months passed before he could return and dig more of the ore. On one of the rare occasions he was able to visit the site, he accidentally encountered a well-armed outlaw camp. The incident discouraged him from returning for nearly two years, and when he did he remained nervous and edgy the entire time.

During one of Payne's infrequent trips to the silver vein, he decided to conceal the presence of the ore so that it would not be discovered by others who chanced to pass this way. He felled several large trees across the creek and constructed a crude dam to divert the path of the flowing water. This done, he covered the vein with rocks and smaller trees. As many times as he had been to the site, he believed he would have no trouble relocating it anytime he wished.

With increasing frequency, Payne's law enforcement assignments and responsibilities took him far from his silver mine for long periods of time. Indian Territory continued to fill with outlaws and other undesirables, and marshals were working longer and harder trying to bring the criminals to justice. Years passed before Payne was able to find an opportunity to return to his secret deposit of ore, but when that opportunity finally arrived he fell ill and was unable to travel.

Payne's illness grew progressively worse. As he lay close to death, he revealed the existence of the vein of silver to a close friend. He described the area near the creek and noted certain landmarks. He also sketched a map showing the location of the site.

Payne never recovered from his illness and died in 1904. Several weeks following his death, the friend decided to make an attempt to locate the vein of silver. Using Payne's map, he ventured into the Ozarks in search of a particular narrow valley with a fast flowing stream. For weeks the friend searched the hills south of Tahlequah but found the map useless. While Payne had been able to ride straight to the creek, he was unable to effectively communicate directions on the map. After several tries, the friend finally gave up and burned the map.

If Joseph Payne was accurate, then somewhere in the low hills in the western region of the Ozark Mountains lies a fortune in almost pure silver. Though Payne extracted silver ore from the vein as often as his responsibilities allowed, he never engaged in full-scale mining, thus no telltale signs of a former mine exist. Others who have grown familiar with this story have searched for the vein of silver but to date no success has ever been recorded.

Some researchers are convinced that Payne's improvised dam across the creek might have rearranged the channel such that the silver may now be buried under several inches of soil.

Today, this region is popular with deer hunters. It is likely that some of them enter Payne's valley in search of game much as Payne did over one hundred years ago in search of outlaws. They may, in fact, be tracking deer across the very layer of soil that covers the lost vein of silver.

W. C. Jameson

Jesse James Gold Cache in the Wichita Mountains

Over the years, the outlaw Jesse James has been associated with more lost and buried treasures than any other individual in history. Very few of these tales carry any level of documentation, and most are pure fiction. Once in a while, however, another Jesse James lost treasure tale comes along and provides compelling reasons to investigate further. The following is such a tale.

During the month of December in 1875, Jesse James and his brother Frank, along with nine other gang members, were believed to have made a journey into the northern part of the Mexican state of Chihuahua. In addition to the two outlaw brothers, the gang was composed of Roy Baxter, Rob Busse (or Bussey), Bud Dalton, Charlie Jones, Frank Miller, George Overton, George Payne, Mack Smith, and Cole Younger. There, according to the lore, the outlaws attacked a burro train transporting an estimated two million dollars worth of gold bullion.

With the fortune in their possession, the gang forded the Rio Grande and re-entered Texas. Following the crossing, they made the long and arduous trip northward, eventually arriving on the first day of March 1876 in the Wichita Mountains in Oklahoma. For three-and-a-half days, the party had traveled through a harsh blizzard. Strong winds made progress difficult. As sundown approached the horses and burros were treading a foot of snow. Jesse suggested they stop for the night and set up camp in the shadow of Tarbone Mountain, located at the eastern end of the range and a short distance from Cache Creek .

The outlaws decided to remain at this site to rest both men and animals until the weather settled. For reasons not entirely clear, Jesse decided the treasure in gold should be cached, explaining that they would return for it later. Near the camp was a small ravine. Into this, the outlaws dumped the treasure, burned the packsaddles, and turned the burros loose to fend for themselves. The gold was covered by caving in the sides of the ravine.

Jesse liked this location so much that he decided to cache additional loot that the gang carried, mostly in the form of gold and silver coins. Using a horseshoe nail, Jesse scratched out a contract onto the metal of an old bucket he found nearby. The agreement bound the eleven outlaws to secrecy relative to the location of the treasure. Each man signed it and the bucket was buried under a ledge on the side of Tarbone Mountain.

Jesse marked the location by hammering a burro shoe onto an oak tree. Walking over to a cottonwood tree a few paces away, he fired twelve pistol shots into the trunk.

Six months later, Jesse and Frank and another version of the gang attempted to rob the bank at Northfield, Minnesota. While Jesse and Frank managed to escape, the others were either killed or captured. Time passed, and the James brothers spent most of their time trying to evade the increased pursuit of law enforcement agencies. By the turn of the century, many of the outlaws who participated in the robbery of the pack train in Chihuahua and the subsequent caching of the gold bullion, including Jesse James, were dead.

At the time, few people knew the story of the caches of gold and other treasures near Tarbone Mountain, and those that did wondered when surviving members of the gang would make an attempt to retrieve it.

In 1903, Cole Younger arrived in the town of Lawton on the southeastern side of the Wichita Mountains. To those who inquired, Younger explained that he was there to establish a newspaper. Younger spent no time at all discussing the possibilities of organizing a newspaper, but was often seen riding his horse in the area of Tarbone Mountain. Those who observed him suggested Younger's excursions appeared as though he were searching for something. On one occasion, Younger asked an area farmer if he had ever seen a tree with a burro shoe nailed to the trunk or another with bullet holes in it. After several days, Younger rode out of Lawton and returned to his home in Lee's Summit, Missouri. He never returned to the region.

In 1907, Frank James purchased a 160-acre farm located between the Wichita Mountains and the Keechi Hills. A few days following the purchase, he, along with his wife Ann, moved to the area. The farm was two miles north of the small town of Fletcher and allegedly near the location where the gold bullion was buried. Within two months after moving to the farm, Frank was visited by Emmett Dalton, a younger brother to Bud Dalton, who had been part of the gang that had robbed the pack train in Mexico.

Like Cole Younger before him, Frank James was often seen riding throughout the region as though searching for something. At the foot of Buzzard Roost Mountain, Frank located and dug up a cache containing $6,000 in gold coins.

Another cache Frank searched for was an old iron teakettle that had been buried with $64,000 worth of gold coins in it. Frank was allegedly in the possession of a cryptic map that purported to show the location of the cache. He was never able to find it.

During the more than three decades that had passed between the caching of the gold bullion and Frank James' arrival in the area, much had changed. Heavy rains and flash floods had reconfigured the drainage patterns across portions of the region. Fires had devastated sections of forests and brush land. Landslides and rockslides had changed the appearance of the slopes of some of the mountains. After seven years of continuous searching, Frank James gave up, sold his farm, and left Oklahoma.

More time passed, and a man named Jim Wilkerson, a former Caddo County deputy sheriff, found a pile of metal buckles and other fittings, the remains, he said, of packsaddles that had long since rotted away. The fittings, said Wilkerson, appeared to have been subjected to a great heat, as from a fire. Though Wilkerson was not aware of it at the time, the James Gang cache of gold bullion resided somewhere under the ground a short distance away.

Another area resident named Joe Hunter spent two decades searching for the various James Gang treasures believed to be hidden in the Wichita Mountains. During one of his forays in the area of Tarbone Mountain, Hunter found the rusted bucket containing the contract Jesse James had scratched into the metal.

Joe Hunter's persistence paid off in another way. One day, he found the iron Teakettle Frank James had for searched so long and hard, the one containing the $64,000 in gold coins. Though never verified, Hunter claimed to have found a tree with a burro shoe nailed to the trunk.

To date, the gold bullion cached by the James Gang has never been found, and it remains a treasure that continues to lure searchers into that region every year.

The Lost Army Payroll

One early morning in June 1892, a stagecoach transporting a United States Army payroll rolled along a well-traveled dirt road toward Fort Sill. The payroll consisted of $100,000 in gold and silver coins. The coach had departed from the station at Wichita Falls, Texas, before sunrise, and as the driver whipped the team of horses northward his only thoughts were of a safe crossing of the Red River and arriving at the fort without mishap. Three days later, he considered, if everything went according to schedule, the coach would reach its destination at the military post. In addition to the driver, the stagecoach carried two guards, each carrying a shotgun and a pistol.

The driver and guards had made this trip several times during the previous months, each time transporting the payroll. Initially, a mounted military escort consisting of six to twelve armed troopers accompanied the coach, but as the months passed and no robbery attempt was ever made, the guards were withdrawn.

On this June morning, however, as the relaxed driver and shotgun-toting guards sat atop the seat of the coach smoking and conversing, three masked riders dashed out from the cover of a stand of trees just off the trail, shot and killed the two lead horses pulling the coach, and wounded one of the guards.

When the coach stopped, one of the outlaws ordered the three men to shed their weapons and jump to the ground. No sooner had the command been given when the second guard raised his shotgun and fired at the mounted bandits, killing two of them. The third outlaw, who was wounded in the shoulder from the blast, shot and killed the guard.

The surviving outlaw then ordered the driver and the wounded guard to lie face down on the ground. Then, he climbed aboard the coach, retrieved the six heavy saddlebags containing the gold and silver coins, and threw them to the ground. As he labored atop the coach, blood leaked from his wound and splattered across the roof of the vehicle.

Dropping to the ground, the outlaw loaded the saddlebags onto the horses belonging to his dead companions. Turning back to the driver and guard, he ordered them to their feet to begin walking back to Wichita Falls. When the two men were out of sight around a bend in the road, the outlaw mounted up, grabbed the reins of the two payroll-laden horses, and set off toward the northeast.

Though he intended to travel to Oklahoma City, the outlaw, suffering intense pain and severe loss of blood from his wound, decided instead to seek medical help. The closest physician, however, was located at Fort Sill. In a daring move, he redirected his route toward the military post.

The outlaw arrived at the fort an hour past sundown on the following day. He reined up near a well located at the side of the trading post. As he watered his horse, he looked around the area for a suitable place to cache the payroll, for he feared that if he were caught with it he would be hung.

After ascertaining that no one was about on this moonless night, the outlaw paced off ten steps from the well, scooped out a hole in the soft soil, and placed the coin-filled saddlebags within. After filling the hole, he walked the horses back and forth over the area to remove any evidence of an excavation. After receiving treatment for his wound, the outlaw decided, he would return to the location, retrieve the payroll, and continue on to Oklahoma City.

An hour later, the outlaw located the post surgeon and told him he had been injured in a hunting accident. He gave his name as Allen. The doctor removed buckshot from the wounds, treated then with antiseptic, and bandaged them. He gave Allen an injection for the pain and invited him to try to get some sleep on the cot in the back office. Weak from loss of blood and exhausted from the long journey, little to no sleep, and the caching of the payroll, Allen lay down on the cot and was asleep within seconds.

As Allen was being treated in the doctor's office, word of the payroll robbery arrived at the fort. Within minutes, six platoons were organized and sent out into the surrounding area to search for some sign of the surviving bandit. At the same time, the driver and the wounded guard were being transported to the fort to provide their account of the robbery.

The next morning, the driver and guard spotted Allen's horse in the post's livery and identified it as belonging to the man who robbed the stagecoach. Allen was roused from his sleep, arrested, and held for trial. He was found guilty and sentenced to prison at Huntsville, Texas. He was to spend the next thirty-three years in confinement.

When Allen was finally released from prison in 1925, he needed to earn a living. He set out to find work. In time, he found a job on a farm at Levelland, a small town in the Texas Panhandle. At the first opportunity, he returned to Fort Sill to try to recover the rich payroll he had buried near the well more than three decades earlier.

When Allen arrived, he found that the military post had changed dramatically. With difficulty, he was able to locate the old trading post and the well adjacent to it. Standing next to the well, it occurred to him that at least two feet of fill dirt had been added to the yard. This, he considered, would make an excavation considerably more difficult than the first time he did it. It also occurred to Allen that he could not remember which direction from the well he had paced off the ten steps. While he was pondering all of this, he was arrested by a military guard for vagrancy and escorted off the post. Allen returned to Levelland, but made plans to make another trip to Fort Sill as soon as possible and attempted to recover the treasure.

Allen's plans to journey back to the military post were interrupted time and again. Several years passed, and though Allen never gave up his ambition to recover the payroll cache, he was unable to find the opportunity to return to Fort Sill. During that time, Allen became close friends with a man named G. W. Cottrell, the owner of a neighboring farm. Allen determined that he could trust Cottrell, so he told him about the robbery of the military payroll and the burying of the coin-filled saddlebags near the well. Allen provided Cottrell directions to the treasure and suggested that he try to find it, explaining that he was too old to do anything with the fortune even if he did recover it. Four months later, Allen died.

Cottrell was seventy-two years old. As soon as his cotton crop was in, he decided to travel to Fort Sill and search for the treasure. He spent several days looking around the post. Finally, he made an appointment to meet with the post historian and librarian, Master Sergeant Morris Swett. Cottrell told Swett his reason for coming to Fort Sill and requested assistance in recovering the payroll. Swett, in turn, introduced Cottrell to a number of officers who requested Cottrell fill out several sets of papers pertinent to his quest and requesting permission to dig for the treasure. This done, the officers suggested that Cottrell return to Levelland and await the results of a military panel that would meet to discuss the matter. Several weeks later, Cottrell was notified that he would be allowed to carry out his search for the payroll.

On January 27, 1937, Cottrell returned to Fort Sill. His first objective was to locate the old well. He learned the old trading post had been torn down and in its place was a maintenance building located at the intersection of McBride and Cureton Streets. The well had been filled in.

Having no notion of which direction from the well the payroll had been buried, Cottrell simply made some guesses related to possible sites. Employing only shovels, Cottrell supervised the excavation of several deep holes a few feet north of the well but found nothing. Cottrell then determined that he needed some heavy earth excavation equipment in order to increase his chances of finding the buried payroll. The U.S. Army was unwilling to allow him to use any military equipment, so the farmer returned to Levelland where he began to make arrangements to lease the equipment and hire some workers to assist him with his search and recovery operation.

As Cottrell was pursuing actions related to the recovery of the treasure, he fell ill. Further, the obligations of running his farming enterprise occupied a great deal of his time. He began to find it more and more difficult to return to Fort Sill to try to recover Allen's lost treasure.

In September, 1940, Cottrell related the story of the cached payroll to a friend named Van Webb and encouraged him to try to fin it. Cottrell wrote Webb a letter of introduction to Fort Sill military officials and even financed his trip to the post. When Webb arrived, however, he was informed he would not be allowed to conduct an excavation and was escorted from the post.

One month later, Cottrell, accompanied by Webb and a woman named Edna Crowder, returned to Fort Sill. Webb employed a divining rod in an attempt to locate the buried payroll. Crowder, who claimed to be a seer and to have mystical powers, consulted a crystal ball for information on the location of the treasure. Neither method was successful and the three returned to Levelland, never to return.

In time, the matter of the buried payroll was forgotten. Then, on April 1, 1964, the U.S. Army announced that it had conducted an investigation and encountered sufficient evidence of the existence of the buried gold and silver coins. The army stated it would make an attempt to recover it.

Employing bulldozers and augurs, army engineers excavated a total of fifteen holes, each of them ten feet deep, and all in an area south of the maintenance building. Nothing was found.

Those who observed and reported on the army's recovery attempt were appalled at what they described as the unprofessional and careless manner in which the search was conducted. They were likewise dismayed that, after excavating a relatively small area, the military completely abandoned the search and refused to allow anyone else to conduct a sophisticated and systematic search for the coins.

Researchers intimate with the story of the buried payroll at Fort Sill are convinced of the truth of Allen's claim. Repeated requests during the past forty years by interested individuals, as well as by treasure recovery professionals, have been denied by military officials. In response to requests to search for the treasure, the army has replied that there is nothing to be gained from renewing search and recovery operations. Skeptics suggest that the military recovered the treasure but refused to acknowledge it, but most researchers are convinced that they failed to locate it.

The refusal of the military to allow others to try to locate the treasure seems bizarre given the amateurish and bungling manner in which they, themselves, attempted search and recovery operations. The truth is, according to researchers, there is much to gain—a fortune in 1890s gold and silver coins.

W. C. Jameson

Lost Mormon Gold Mine in the Spavinaw Hills

During the early part of the nineteenth century, Pryor, Oklahoma, was a young town in search if its own personality and future. On the one hand, it had become a gathering place for outlaws who found it an ideal location from which to range out and commit various crimes. Shootings were common in Pryor during that time, as were knifings, robberies, and other felonious acts.

On the other hand, despite the tarnishing of the town's reputation by the lawless element, the civic leaders boasted that it was an example of a progressive and thriving young urban area in Oklahoma. The Chamber of Commerce, in an effort to lure businesses and new residents to the area, publicized the beauty of the nearby Oklahoma hills, the pleasant weather, its colorful history, and more.

One of the aspects of Pryor that was pointed to with pride at every available opportunity was the Pryor Orphans' Home. Though times were difficult economically and many were without work, the home remained open as a result of generous donations from citizens and churches.

Much of the success of the Pryor Orphans' Home was due to the work and leadership of Reverend W. T. Whittaker. Whittaker founded and oversaw the operation of the orphanage, and it was largely due to his persuasive and persistent manner that the institution was able to keep its doors open. When not on site at the home, Whittaker traveled throughout the town and the countryside soliciting donations of money, clothing, food, and even labor related to the maintenance and upkeep of buildings and grounds. Whittaker was a tireless worker, seldom taking a day off from what he considered his principal mission.

On a spring morning in 1921, Whittaker stopped by the post office to mail some letters. When he picked up his own mail he found an envelope with an Ohio postmark. Curious, he tore it open and read the letter.

The writer, an Ohio resident, explained to Whittaker that he had been given his name and address by a person who assured him of the reverend's honesty and credibility. The writer also stated that his source had also informed him that Whittaker was familiar with the geography of the nearby Spavinaw Hills region of the Ozarks and that his knowledge could be helpful. Following this introduction, the letter continued with an interesting story.

The writer of the letter told Whittaker that he had recently learned of the existence of a rich gold mine in the Spavinaw Hills, located a short distance east of Pryor. He also claimed he was in possession of maps of the area and would pay Whittaker a large sum of money if he would guide the Ohioan into the region, help him locate the mine, and provide him with men to help dig out the gold.

Whittaker decided to accept the Ohioan's offer, seeing in it an opportunity to acquire a significant amount of money to help the cause of the orphanage. Whittaker raced home and penned a reply agreeing to the proposition and requesting additional details.

Several weeks later, Whittaker received a reply from the Ohioan. The man explained that he had come into possession of the diary of a man who had worked in the gold mine many years earlier. The man was one of twelve Mormons who had been exploring the area in search of a suitable location to move their families and establish a settlement. They arrived in a valley in the Spavinaw Hills that held promise and potential for growing crops and grazing cattle. While studying the area, they discovered a rich vein of gold quite by accident in an outcrop of weathered granite that had been exposed from the surrounding limestone. Convinced they had been sent by God to find this gold and take it for their church, the Mormons established a tiny settlement and bent to the task of mining and smelting the ore. When they had accumulated a significant amount, they intended to transport it to church headquarters at Salt Lake City where it would be used to fund the construction of the temple.

Day after day from dawn until late in the evening the men worked in the mine, stopping only to rest, eat, sleep, and conduct worship services. Over time they removed tons of rock, enlarging and extending a shaft that pierced the hillside. The ore was separated from the matrix, crudely smelted, and processed into eighteen-inch-long ingots.

Following several months of hard work, the Mormons had accumulated several hundred bars of gold that they stacked along one wall of the mineshaft. They intended to purchase a string of mules to transport the gold to Utah once the mine was exhausted.

During their mining activities, the remote Mormon community was visited from time to time by outlaws. For the most part, the newcomers, on seeing the poor appearance of the tiny settlement, concluded there was nothing worth stealing and soon went on their way. During other visits, robbery at gunpoint occurred. On at least two occasions a gunfight erupted between would-be bandits and the Mormons.

Because such incidents were increasing, and because the leaders of the Mormon settlement began to fear for the safety of their families, they decided the time had come to close the mine and depart for Utah. In the future when the military and various law enforcement agencies had become established in the region and subdued the criminal element of eastern Oklahoma, they intended to return and resume the mining activities. Before leaving, the Mormons loaded a few of the gold ingots into their wagons. They left most of them inside the shaft. They then covered the mine and camouflaged it to look much like the adjacent hillside.

For reasons never ascertained, the Mormons did not return to the Spavinaw Hills to reclaim their gold. Years passed, and the story of the lost Mormon gold mine came into the possession of the letter writer via a journal that had been kept by one of the miners.

Convinced of the authenticity of the tale and the existence of the gold mine, Whittaker spent the next few days recruiting men to accompany him and the Ohioan on an expedition into the Spavinaw Hills. Once this had been arranged, Whittaker decided to write to the Ohioan and explain that everything was ready to proceed and that he should come to Pryor at the first opportunity.

On his way home to pen the important letter, however, Whittaker suffered a heart attack. The reverend lay in a coma for several days, unable to speak or move. Days later, in the presence of friends and family, he died.

Several weeks following Whittaker's death, family members discovered the correspondence between him and the man from Ohio. Unaware that the Ohioan was awaiting a letter from Whittaker summoning him to Pryor, the matter was ignored. It is presumed that the Ohioan believed the reverend had no time for or interest in the matter and decided not to pursue further communication.

Over the next several years, the story of the mine, now called The Lost Mormon Gold Mine, surfaced from time to time. Men occasionally entered the Spavinaw Hills in search of the mine and the huge cache of gold ingots believed to reside within. On one of these explorations, a small party of searchers found the remains of an old settlement in a remote valley. Convinced this was what was left of the community established by the Mormons, they searched the area and later came upon a primitive smelter. More days of searching, however, failed to located the abandoned mine.

More time passed. The city of Tulsa, responding to the growing need for an improved and more dependable water resource undertook the development of plans to create a reservoir on the Neosho River to be used as a water supply for the city. Once the dam was constructed, water backed up into several of the secluded valleys of the Spavinaw Hills.

Most of the researchers who have studied The Lost Mormon Gold Mine are convinced that the actual site of the mine was subsequently submerged when the valleys were filled to form Spavinaw Lake. A team of four professional treasure hunters have examined the possibility of locating the old mine shaft, reopening it, and recovering the gold they believe lies within. The effort would require the use of SCUBA gear and underwater recovery techniques, but all involved with this adventure regarded the objective as attainable. At this writing, discussions relating to the recovery continue.

W. C. Jameson

Lost Spanish Treasure in the Wichita Mountains

The five riders carefully guided their mounts along the canyon floor, picking their way through rock and rubble that had eroded from the mountainsides eons ago, pulled by gravity to lower levels. The men rode in silence as they constantly scanned the ridge tops. They were on the lookout for two things: Indians and landmarks. During the early to middle part of the nineteenth century, Comanches still roamed and raided throughout Oklahoma's Wichita Mountains. The landmarks, the riders believed, would lead them to a huge fortune in Spanish gold cached long ago in this portion of the range.

As the party of riders exited this canyon they spotted another, a smaller one that they were convinced was the place they were searching for. The leader, a rancher who ran cattle on the nearby plains, called for a halt. Seated in the saddle, he withdrew a folded parchment from his saddlebag, opened it, and examined it with great care. He informed his companions that, according to the map, a long lost underground vault constructed by Spanish miners was located a short distance ahead. Taking another long look at the surroundings, the leader refolded the map and returned it to his saddlebag. He spurred his mount forward and the others followed. The anticipation of locating and recovering the lost fortune in Spanish gold exceeded only their apprehension of what might happen to them should they be discovered by the Comanches. The band of Indians currently residing in the range had been blamed for several recent raids, the killing of settlers and travelers, and the burnings of a number of ranch houses and barns.

Days prior to departing on the expedition to locate the lost caches of gold, the leader of the party had invited the other four men to his home, outlined his objective, and explained the circumstances that provided him with the motive for a search.

Ten months earlier, he said, he had encountered an elderly Mexican man wandering the periphery of the Wichita Mountains. The rancher approached him and learned that he was lost, had been out of food and water for days, was delirious, and on the verge of collapse. He transported the man to his ranch house and nursed him back to health. After the Mexican had rested for three days, he told the rancher that he had come from the Mexican state of Jalisco. He was looking for a shaft that was reputed to conceal hundreds of gold ingots that had been stacked and left behind when Spanish miners were forced to flee the area because of increasing deadly raids by Comanches.

The rancher expressed some skepticism about such a tale. Anxious to prove the truth of his mission, the Mexican removed a large, folded band of silk from around his waist and spread it out on the dining table. Embroidered on the silk was a map showing the location of the treasure shaft along with several prominent landmarks, many of which were recognized by the rancher. When questioned by the Mexican, the rancher explained that the map seemed to be accurate and he indicated where certain landmarks could be found.

The rancher explained to the Mexican that the threat of Comanches was still viable and warned him against traveling alone and unarmed in the range. Undaunted, the following morning, well fed and well rested, the Mexican thanked the rancher and walked away toward the Wichita Mountains. Days later, he returned to the ranch house. He explained that while searching for the landmarks, he spotted Indians on several occasions and was forced to lay up in hiding for hours at a time.

The rancher was becoming convinced of the existence of the lost treasure in gold, but he repeatedly warned the Mexican about the dangers of risking his life in the Wichita Mountains wilderness. Following several more attempts to locate the treasure, the Mexican told the rancher that he was beginning to believe that he was not destined to find it. He thanked the rancher for his hospitality and told him that he would return to Mexico on the morrow. Before leaving, he asked the rancher how he might repay him for his kindnesses. The rancher replied that he would like to be allowed to make a copy of the map. That evening, the two men reproduced the geography, distances, and directions from the silk to a piece of parchment. The Mexican departed at dawn of the following day and was never seen in the area again.

The more the rancher studied the map, the more he became familiar enough with the Wichita Mountains to have a fine chance of locating the treasure cache. He waited until the following spring, assembled his four neighbors, and told them about the existence of the treasure. He said they needed to enter the range well armed, for the threat of the Comanches had not diminished. All four of the men agreed to participate.

Now, seated upon their horses at the entrance to the small canyon, the rancher explained to them that, if the map was accurate, the treasure was not far away and that they should have their hands on it in a matter of a few hours. Following the directions, a short time later they arrived at a location where an excavation had apparently been undertaken in the floor of the canyon a long time go and then subjected to an effort of concealment.

After posting one of the men on a nearby ridge to maintain a lookout for Comanches, the others unstrapped picks and shovels from their horses and began to dig. They excavated five feet of fill dirt and rocks from the shaft. Once the fill was removed, they encountered a three-foot-tall man-made rock-and-mortar barrier on one wall of the passageway. Employing their tools, they tore down the wall to reveal the opening to a second shaft that sloped downward at a thirty-degree angle.

Inside this shaft the air was cool and musty, and near the entrance they found several old mining tools and a few bones that appeared to be human. The men were forced to fashion torches before entering the dark tunnel to find their way. A few yards inside this second tunnel, they were stunned to find hundreds of stacked gold bars. Each bar was eighteen-inches-long and quite heavy. On the floor at the end of the ingots were a number of partially rotted woven baskets, each containing hundreds of gold coins, all with Spanish markings. Beyond the baskets was a large pile of leather pouches. As one of the men was preparing to slice open a pouch, they heard a shout from their companion who was standing guard on the ridge.

The men crawled out of the shaft and stared up at the ridge where they saw the guard pointing toward the north and signaling the approach of Comanches. He said they were a few miles away but approaching rapidly. The men scrambled to the top of the ridge for a look. In the distance they could make out the riders and trailing a cloud of dust. They estimated one hundred warriors were riding toward them. They ran back down the slope, mounted their horses, and galloped out of the small canyon and as fast as possible.

The five men rode for an hour. They took shelter in a secluded canyon that afforded decent protection behind large boulders in case the Indians tracked them and attacked. They remained until noon of the following day. Then they decided to venture out and take their chances on a return to the gold. With extreme caution they made their way back to the small canyon. On arriving, they found that the Comanches had refilled the shaft. Unwilling to attempt a second excavation while the danger of being discovered was high, the men decided to return to their ranches and await for a more propitious time to re-enter the area.

When the leader returned home, he discovered that he had lost the map, apparently during the flight from the Indians. Without the map, he was not certain he could relocate the canyon. He did not have the opportunity to find out for several years, as the Indian menace continued making it hazardous to any and all who ventured into the territory. More time passed, and the Civil War began to consume the attention of the nation. The rancher and his neighbors were called to serve. Some of them never returned to Oklahoma, and those that did never took up a renewed search for the lost Spanish treasure.

Another party of men attempted to look for the lost treasure cache. It is unknown how they learned of it, but they apparently arrived in the same location as the five ranchers. While they were excavating the shaft, according to the tale, they were attacked by Comanches and killed.

A few things can be assumed about the role of the Comanches as it relates to this lost treasure in the Wichita Mountains. Some are convinced that the Indians were guarding the cache, but most experts don't agree. The Comanches had little use for gold and other precious metals save for the occasional fashioning of ornaments. When they became aware of the white man's lust for the shiny metal and learned what it could purchase, Comanches and other Indian tribes often mined small amounts of gold and used it to purchase rifles, ammunition, and supplies. In the case of the lost Spanish gold in the Wichita range, it is more likely that the Indians resented the trespass of the white men and were more intent on keeping them out of their territory, and in the case of this particular range, their holy places.

The Comanches knew that if the white men were aware of gold in the Wichita Mountains they would arrive in great numbers in a short time and, as they had done so many times before elsewhere, displace the Indians who lived there. It is believed there were, in fact, a number of Spanish gold mines in the Wichita Mountains. Most researchers agree that, in most cases, the Spaniards were driven out of the region and the Comanches, sealed off, covered, and disguised gold and silver mines in an attempt to keep others from finding them.

The Comanche, as well as the Kiowa, who still live in the area of the Wichita Mountains today, relate tales of the ghosts of their ancestors who roam the range, watching over the ancient territory and, in some cases, protecting the old gold mines and any other treasures that were buried there. In recent years, treasure hunters who have entered the range have reported spotting strange lights along the ridge tops as well as hearing unidentifiable sounds coming from deep underground. These mysterious occurrences remain unsolved

Lost Mines and Buried Treasures of Oklahoma

Lost Mexican Gold Ingots

For decades prior to the Civil War, the Great Plains of the United Stats was crisscrossed with dozens of major and minor travel and transportation routes. Along these routes moved trappers, traders, peddlers, Indians, soldiers, settlers, miners, and others. Many of the miners who found, excavated, and processed precious ore from the Colorado Rocky Mountains often utilized these roads to transport their bullion to St. Louis, New Orleans, and other destinations. Sometimes the gold was converted to cash or traded for important goods and supplies. Occasionally it was loaded onto ships and carried across the gulf to a port in eastern Mexico.

It has been estimated by historians that many millions of dollars worth of gold and sometimes silver were hauled across the plains to the growing business centers along the Mississippi River. Some of the caravans carrying gold, however, never made it to intended destinations. As a result of depredation by Indians and bandits, along with other mishaps including bad weather and floods, some was lost, stolen, hidden in caches, or abandoned along the way.

In 1849, a party of Mexican miners loaded a large accumulation of gold ingots onto twenty-six burros. Following several years of mining and smelting the gold at a location in the Rocky Mountains in southern Colorado, they made ready to depart. They intended to convert their metal into cash and return to their homeland and their families where they planned to establish fine ranches and raise blooded cattle and horses. After strapping the gold onto packsaddles, lashing these to the burros, and loading all of their belongings into three heavy ox carts, they set out for New Orleans. They would take a ship to the port of Vera Cruz on the east coast of Mexico. It was spring when the party arrived in Santa Fe, New Mexico. Here, the Mexicans purchased supplies to see them on their long journey across the Texas Panhandle and into Oklahoma, a route they had earlier selected to New Orleans.

Long days of travel ensued, and the journey was, for the most part, uneventful until they arrived at a location in what is today Roger Mills County in far western Oklahoma. As the pack train crested a low hill on the prairie and the leader looked for a suitable place to set up camp for the night, one of the drag riders screamed a warning – Indians were approaching from the north and they appeared intent on attack. Ill prepared for such an event, the Mexicans' first impulse was to flee. Unable to goad the oxen to greater speeds, the miners, in their haste to get away, simply abandoned them and the carts. They concentrated on herding the gold-laden burros to some defensible position.

Descending the low hill, the leader of the group spotted a stream a short distance away. The stream meandered in an almost complete circle, nearly enclosing a slightly elevated sandy neck of land. Believing they might be able to hold off the Indians there, the Mexicans headed toward it, whipping the struggling burros along as they went.

Seconds after arriving at a point near the end of the neck, several of the Mexicans dismounted and, loading their flintlocks, faced the oncoming Indians. The others worked to maintain control of the frightened burros and horses.

The Indians, recognized by the Mexicans as Comanches, stopped at the entrance to the narrow slice of land nearly surrounded by the ox-bow meander of the stream. As it was only moments before sundown, the Indians, choosing not to fight in the dark, retreated a short distance away and established a camp of their own.

The Mexicans mistakenly believed that the Indians were after the gold they were transporting, unaware that the Comanches were responding, for the most part, to the trespass across their traditional lands. The leader made the decision to bury the gold, leave the burros for the Indians, and return at a later time to retrieve their fortune. For the next hour, the men excavated a wide shallow hole near the end of the sandy neck of land into which they deposited the ingots. This done, they turned the burros loose, mounted up, crossed the stream, and rode away in the darkness.

At dawn, the Comanches arrived at the neck and discovered their quarry was gone. Locating the tracks of the miners, the Indians set out in pursuit. Later that same day, the warriors overtook the party and slew all but two men who managed to escape. Weeks later, the survivors of the massacre arrived in New Orleans to tell the tale of what had occurred on the Oklahoma prairie and the buried treasure in gold ingots. At the time, the men feared returning to the plains of western Oklahoma and encountering the Comanches. Thus the matter of the buried gold was soon forgotten.

In 1890, an Indian walked into the Cheyenne-Arapaho Agency Trading Post located near the Washita River. After selecting a sack full of groceries and other items, he attempted to pay with a heavy gold bar that he handed to the proprietor. The ingot was crudely smelted, was later estimated to be ninety percent pure gold, and was worth many times more than the goods the Indian wished to purchase. The proprietor recognized the ingot for what it was and asked the Indian where he had obtained it.

The Indian, a Comanche, explain that he had dug it out of the ground on what he called a small island on White Shield Creek. The term "island" was often used to identify an extension of land surrounded by an ox-bow meander. The Comanche stated that, from time to time when he needed to buy something, he would go to the island, dig up one of the gold ingots that he knew the white men liked, and trade it for goods. He also said there were hundreds more buried at the same location. He said that, according to a tale told in his tribe, a group of Mexicans was massacred near that location by a war party led by his grandfather. Before the Mexicans were killed, he said, they buried the shiny metal on the island.

As the proprietor questioned the Indian in an attempt to obtain more information on the location of the buried gold ingots, the Indian grew suspicious and left. He was never seen in the trading post again.

The proprietor set his sights on locating and retrieving the immense fortune in gold he was certain was buried on a neck of land near White Shield Creek. He recruited several friends and traveled to Carpenter Town (today called Carpenter), a small settlement ten miles northeast of Elk City and not far from White Shield Creek. Standing atop a hill that overlooked the creek, the men found the remains of three ox carts along with some trace fittings and other items. East of the hill was the creek. In plain view was the exaggerated meander, called a gooseneck by the proprietor. The men rode to the "island," excavated a few holes at random locations, but found nothing. Impatient men become discouraged easily, and annoyed at not finding any treasure, they gave up and returned to the agency.

Since that search for the gold ingots, only one concentrated effort has been undertaken to find the buried treasure. A man who spent considerable time researching the story of the buried Mexican ingots and studying every piece of information related to it he could locate, confided in a few friends that he was convinced he knew where it was and could find it. The year was 1960.

Using topographic maps published by the United States Geological Survey, the researcher studied the area thoroughly. He even deduced a logical route that would have been taken by the Mexican miners on their journey from Santa Fe to New Orleans one hundred years earlier.

According to the researcher's calculations, White Shield Creek was located a few hundred yards from a low ridge, the one he was convinced was the location where the Mexicans first spotted the approaching Comanches. In a letter the researcher composed to his wife, he stated that he climbed the ridge and, from this vantage point, spotted the great curve in the stream. Just beyond the channel, he described an old railroad bed that ran in a north-south direction. Just to the east of that, he wrote, was State Highway 34, close enough, he said, to hear the sound of traffic along the route.

After arriving at the neck of land within the meander, the researcher continued in his letter, he claimed that he had found the buried gold ingots and that they were less than one mile from the highway. In closing, he said he was going to travel to Elk City, rent a large truck, and return to the area and park the vehicle as close to the site as possible and recover the gold.

At Elk City, the researcher purchased a stamp at the post office and mailed the letter. He then located a vehicle rental agency and made arrangements for the use of a commercial van with heavy-duty suspension. By the time his transaction was complete, it was early evening. He decided to check into an inexpensive motel, get a good night's sleep, and commence his plans to recover the gold early in the morning.

Following breakfast, the researcher drove the van along Highway 34 toward a pre-selected point where he intended to park while he gathered the gold ingots. At 9:45 a.m., he was killed in a head-on collision with a pick-up truck pulling a four-horse trailer.

Two days later, his wife received the letter. In spite of the directions to the treasure contained in the missive, the widow never undertook a search for the gold. Months passed, and on several occasions the widow was contacted by men who professed an interest in the treasure. They explained they wished to make an attempt at recovering the gold, promising a share to her if she would reveal the information gleaned by her late husband. While the widow listened politely to all of the treasure seekers and their offers, she ultimately refused to share any of the information contained in the letter.

To date, as far as anyone knows, no other formal search and recovery of the treasure in Mexican gold ingots buried next to White Shield Creek has been undertaken.

In recent years, a new element has been added to this tale. A few who have studied the tale of the buried Mexican gold ingots are convinced that the location now lies beneath the water of Foss Reservoir, an impoundment east of the town of Carpenter. Should this be the case, it is important to know that the lake is fairly shallow and, should the location of the cache ever be identified within its limits, an underwater recovery is not only possible, but well within the abilities of even the most novice SCUBA diver.

The Cobbler's Gold Cache

In the summer of 1870, an elderly German arrived in the northeastern part of Indian Territory on foot. He traveled alone save for the company of two mules carrying his belongings. The German's ragged, dirty, and trail-worn appearance suggested that he had been on the road for a long time. Even the mules looked weary and haggard from transporting their heavy burdens.

The old man stopped at farmhouses when he encountered them and offered to work in return for food, some grain for his mules, and a place to sleep. He told everyone that he was a cobbler. In a short time he found plenty of work mending the boots and shoes of the area's residents.

The old man was friendly and got along well with everyone, but preferred to be alone. At times, he appeared secretive, always looking about to see if anyone was watching him. When anyone approached his mules he would chase them away. If someone came near his heavy packs he suggested they be on their way. Then he would examine his possessions to make certain they had not been tampered with. Once, as the old German was repacking one of his mules, he pulled out several leather sacks, opened them, and counted the contents – gold coins. He was spotted by a farmer, and in a short time others in the area became aware of the old man's riches.

The German had been in the region for several weeks when he decided to establish a residence on a parcel of land fronting the Spring River a few miles northeast of present-day Miami, Oklahoma. There were no other white residents nearby, the closest neighbors being a few members of the Piankashaw tribe, a small group of Indians that had been moved into the Territory only three years earlier as part of a government relocation program.

The cobbler built a crude cabin from native materials, mostly logs and rocks. He spurned offers for help. Anyone who chanced to drop by the cobbler's new residence were always greeted in a friendly manner but never encouraged to remain for long. The German remained secretive and never allowed anyone to enter his dwelling.

One day as the cobbler was visiting a nearby settlement and purchasing some items at a trading post, he was spotted by a traveler who later related to area residents that he had known the old man in Germany. He claimed the cobbler had come from a wealthy and influential family, but for unknown reasons chose to become a cobbler and travel from village to village repairing footwear. After earning his living in this manner for several years, the cobbler departed for the United States. He landed on the east coast and immediately set out for the West. He worked his way across the country on foot performing odd jobs and cobbling. During his travels he acquired the two mules he still possessed. Most of the people he encountered described him as friendly and eccentric but harmless. The traveler also claimed that the cobbler carried much of his family's wealth with him when he came to America.

Aside from his infrequent visits to the trading post, few people encountered the cobbler except for some of the Piankashaw Indians that were his neighbors. The cobbler became close friends with one young member of the tribe and occasionally invited him to share a meal. One day, as the two were seated on the ground in front of the cabin, the cobbler confided in the Indian that he possessed a great wealth in gold coins. He showed the young man a large tin box in which he claimed most of his fortune was kept and confessed to him that he was unable to sleep at night for fear that someone would rob him of his treasure. The Indian suggested that he hide the box of coins someplace where no one could find it.

The old cobbler considered this for several days and decided to follow the advice of the Indian. For days thereafter, he explored the area around his cabin in search of a suitable place and finally found one.

Near a point where Rock Creek flows into the Spring River, a high limestone bluff contained several deep and narrow crevices along its face. Entering one of these openings, the German followed the cave for a distance until it became too dark to see. Fashioning a torch from grasses that grew along the creek, he re-entered the crevice and inched forward on his stomach for a few yards. The cobbler followed the passageway until he came to a large opening in which he was able to stand. Here in the chamber far from prying eyes, he decided to cache his fortune.

The next morning, the cobbler transported the coins by mule to a point near the crevice. It took several trips, but he finally succeeded in carrying all of the coins to the secret hiding place. He arranged the tin box in one corner of the chamber and filled it with the sacks of coins. He then covered this treasure with dirt, making it difficult to spot should anyone venture this deep in the crevice.

Days later when the cobbler encountered the young Indian, he informed him that he had hidden his treasure where no one would ever find it, and that he had slept peacefully for the first time in months.

Another year passed, and the old German grew weak with pneumonia. He was often racked with fits of coughing and remained confined to his bed. He was unable to go about his daily chores, and the simple act of preparing a meal left him exhausted.

The cobbler's young Indian friend arrived for a visit and brought him some broth. When the old man did not respond to his knock on the door, the Indian entered the cabin and found the old man lying in his bed and near death. Raising a feeble hand, the German pulled the Pianakashaw closer and, in a halting and breathless voice, told him that before he died he wanted to reveal the location of his fortune in gold coins. He explained to the Indian that he wanted him to have his wealth for being such a loyal friend and for caring for him during his sickness. He told the Indian to use the money to benefit the tribe.

Before a week passed, the old man was dead. The Piankashaw buried him next to his cabin and conducted a simple service in the manner of Indians.

Following the burial, the Indian set out to find the cobbler's gold coins. He traveled to the confluence of Rock Creek and the Spring River and spotted the limestone bluff described the old man. In searching the area, the Piankashaw encountered numerous crevices, explored them, but found none that contained the coins. Over and over the young Indian looked for the treasure but it always eluded him. After months of searching with no success, he finally gave up. The story of the cobbler' gold coins was passed along in the tribe for well over a century.

In 1979, a Kiowa Indian named Weldon Bobcat spent a lot of time in the area of the Spring River. Bobcat hunted wild game, fished, and trapped. He brought most of the meat home to his family and sold the rest to area residents. After tanning the hides of the coyotes, wild cats, and raccoons he trapped, he marketed them though a hide broker. Weldon Bobcat provided a decent living for his family.

Once when interviewed for a newspaper article, Bobcat related an interesting story. He recalled that several young boys had been playing around Devil's Promenade a few years earlier when one of them entered a narrow crevice in the face of the bluff. Crawling flat on his stomach, the youth discovered that the low cave extended for several yards. When he finally came out, he told his companions that the passageway continued into the bluff for a long way and eventually opened up into a chamber large enough to accommodate several people. He confessed to being afraid of the numerous spiders he encountered and said he did not care to go back.

Many are convinced that the boy accidentally discovered the long lost location of the old German cobbler's treasure in gold coins. Unaware of the legend passed down by the Indians, there was no reason for him to consider that he might have been within inches of a fortune.

The Buried Military Gold Shipment

During the late 1890s, an elderly man arrived in St. Joseph, Missouri, having walked a great distance. His shoes were coming apart and his clothes appeared as though they had been slept in many times. The old man, carrying only a small pack, walked through the wide, heavy doors of a livery stable and watched as the owner fed the riding stock boarded there. Politely, the stranger waited for the owner to finish his chores, then stepped forward and offered to work for some food and perhaps a bit of money.

The livery owner could see that the old man was sick and weak. He took the newcomer to his house and fed him. Following dinner, he told the stranger he was welcome to sleep in one of the empty stalls at the livery. When he was feeling better, said the owner, he could do a few chores around the business.

The next morning, the livery owner assigned some light duties to the old man, but he passed out twice before lunch. The second time he regained consciousness, he was racked with a deep and harsh cough. A physician was summoned, and he diagnosed the old man as suffering from a case of advanced tuberculosis. The livery owner told the old man to rest in one of the stalls and not be concerned about the chores until he recovered from his malady.

Each day, however, the old man grew weaker. The compassionate livery owner continued to feed and care for him. His offers to have him carried to the nearest hospital were refused by the old man who said he did not trust doctors. More time passed, and it was clear that he was dying. The livery owner did everything he could to make his last days as comfortable as possible.

One evening as the livery owner was finishing up his work and preparing to return home, the old man summoned him to his side and told him he wanted to repay him for his kindness. Then he related an amazing story.

The old man said a few months before arriving in St. Joseph he had been released from prison after serving twenty years for his part in a robbery. The gang he was a member of, he explained, had stolen a military payroll shipment. They had killed the driver of the wagon and every member of the armed escort.

Early one cold winter dawn in 1869, the gang of seventeen outlaws had been waiting in hiding in a grove of trees next to Mill Creek, a small stream that flowed through a portion of south-central Oklahoma. The bandits were waiting for the arrival of a wagon transporting a large military payroll in gold coins along with three wagons carrying supplies and weapons. The party had left Fort Leavenworth, Kansas, days earlier and was bound for Fort Arbuckle. Before long, the outlaws could hear the approach of the wagon and riders. As the caravan slowed while rounding a bend a short distance up the trail, the outlaws unleashed a barrage of rifle fire, killing most of the soldiers with the first volley. Following a brief firefight, the remaining troopers were killed along with five of the outlaws.

The bandits broke into the payroll wagon, removed the large shipment of gold coins, and loaded it onto several mules. This done, they pulled the wagon into a tight circle and set them on fire in an attempt to create the impression to any pursuing cavalry that Indians were responsible. As the wagons burned, the outlaws, leading the gold-laden mules, galloped away.

After riding for several hours along a route that roughly paralleled Mill Creek, the outlaws stopped next to the narrow stream, unloaded the payroll, and divided it into three piles. Two of the piles were placed in heavy sacks and cooking pots and buried in two separate locations next to the bank. They placed the contents of the third pile into empty coffee cans and loaded them back onto the mules. Setting a course due north, they continued riding toward the Arbuckle Mountains.

Two nights later the twelve surviving outlaws were encamped in the mouth of a cave in the Arbuckles. Before continuing their flight, they decided to bury the coffee cans in the loose dirt in the floor of the cave. Following this, they decided to split up into three groups and ride off in different directions in order to confuse any pursuing troopers. They made arrangements to meet in two months at a selected location. From there, they would return to the cave near the small creek and retrieve the gold coins.

One of three groups, led by a Mexican, rode south. They intended to go into Mexico and await word. A second group rode toward Arkansas. The third group, of which the old man had been a member, rode northeastward planning to hide out in Missouri. The pursuing cavalry, however, picked up their trail. Aided by area law enforcement officers, they caught up with this group of outlaws. Following a brief gun battle, all of the bandits were killed save for the old man who was captured. He was tried and sentenced to prison for his part in the robbery. He stated during his trial that he had no part in killing any of the soldiers and was only holding the mules as the robbery was taking place.

While serving his time in prison, the old man learned that his companions who had traveled to Arkansas had all been killed. Nothing was ever heard from the party that went to Mexico.

As the dying stranger related this strange tale to the livery owner, he sketched a map on a piece of butcher paper showing the location where the robbery occurred, the location of Fort Arbuckle, and the three sites where the gold coins had been buried. By the time he got this far in his story, he was seized by another fit of coughing and was unable to continue. By the time the attack had subsided, the old man was so weakened that he lay down to sleep. Two days later he was dead.

The livery owner was convinced of the truth of the old man's tale. After thinking about the possibilities of finding the buried gold coins, he decided to go in search of them. A few days later he sold his livery stable and headed south into Oklahoma.

Weeks later the liveryman arrived in the town of Davis, the only settlement of any size in the general vicinity of where the dying man said the gold had been buried. Following the map, he was able to relate certain critical landmarks to the notations the old man had sketched on the map. Once he arrived at the indicated sites of the burials along Mill Creek, however, the directions grew vague and he became disoriented. He dug at several spots he considered promising but found nothing.

The liveryman's search for the buried coins continued for months. Though experiencing no success, or even encouragement, he refused to give up. He was convinced that the dying man in his livery stable had been telling the truth and that sooner or later he would find the treasure.

In time, the liveryman ran out of money and was forced to take a job in Davis. He constructed a simple one-room log cabin on a low hill just outside of town, married a local Indian woman, and dedicated all of his free time to searching for the buried payroll.

Months of searching turned into years. The once-successful liveryman now grew old, partially blind, and was nearly penniless. It grew more and more difficult for him to conduct his searches, but he persisted. In 1930 his wife left him. He sometimes went several days without food. By this time the citizens of Davis regarded him as a demented old man and placed no credence in his story of the buried payroll.

The liveryman had one friend in Davis. Samuel Davis, the founder of the town and a leading merchant in the area, was fond of the old liveryman and enjoyed visiting with him and listening to his stories of his search for the buried treasure. Davis would occasionally bring food to the old man at his cabin. Knowing how important it was to him, Davis encouraged him to continue searching for the gold.

When the liveryman became too old and infirm to continue his searches, he gave the now weathered treasure map to Davis and wished him good luck.

Davis had always been impressed by the old man's unshakeable belief in the existence of the gold and was convinced it could be found. When time permitted, he would take the old map and spend days at a time searching the area around Mill Creek.

One afternoon Davis was visiting a rancher through whose property flowed Mill Creek where two of the caches were reputed to be located. To Davis' surprise, the rancher told him that on occasions in the past, a party of men would approach him and request permission to camp along the creek. Only one month earlier, said the rancher, a group of five Mexicans arrived at his house and inquired about camping along the creek to do some fishing. The rancher obliged them but grew suspicious when he saw no fishing gear whatsoever. Instead, the men carried picks and shovels.

A few days after the Mexicans had departed, the rancher walked down to the creek where they had been camped. About forty yards from the campsite he found several holes dug into the creek bank. Lying beside one of the holes was an old iron cook pot that had apparently been buried for many years. The rancher told Davis that he saw impressions of coins in the dirt at the bottom of the pot.

Davis suspected that the Mexicans may have had a connection to the group of outlaws that rode south following the robbery and the caching of the payroll in 1869. He presumed they possessed directions to at least one of the cache sites, but Davis believed they would have returned to Mexico after locating the first one. Davis was convinced the other two caches were still where they had been buried in 1869 and that they could still be found.

When he could find the time, Davis spent portions of the next several years in search of the gold coins. Eventually, the press of his businesses precluded his continued effort and he reluctantly abandoned the search. He placed the old map in a room in his home. Years later when he went to look for it he was unable to find it.

Another Davis resident, a seasoned treasure hunter with over three decades of experience, also believed in the existence of the lost gold payroll and dedicated considerable time and effort in search of it. He was convinced that the payroll was buried not on Mill Creek, but on the banks of Guy Sandy Creek. He claimed he could prove this contention, but when asked to do so was never forthcoming with any evidence of such. Unfortunately relative to the recovery of the buried gold coins, the portion of Guy Sandy Creek along which it was purportedly buried, he claims, is now under fifty feet of water. In 1962, the Lake of the Arbuckles was created as a result of the construction of a dam at the confluences of Rock Creek, Buckhorn Creek, and Guy Sandy Creek.

As for the cache allegedly buried in a cave in the Arbuckle Mountains, nothing has been learned. No one is clear about which route the outlaws took through the range as they fled from pursuing cavalry. Furthermore, there are hundreds of caves in the Arbuckle Mountains, and the task of searching all of them would be imposing.

Still, the chances are great that a fortune in the gold payroll coins minted circa 1869 still lies under a thin cover of dirt in one of these caves. It may be only a matter of time before they are found.

Devil's Canyon Gold

Devil's Canyon is located at the extreme western end of the Wichita Mountain range of Oklahoma. It is a southwest-northeast oriented cut in the rock flanked by Flat Top Mountain and Soldiers' Peak. The steep walls of the two mountains keep much of the canyon in shade during the day, lending a dark and forbidding atmosphere to the rocky, brush-choked floor of the gorge.

There are legends associated with Devil's Canyon. One of them relates that the canyon has long been haunted by the spirits of the many men who died there. Indeed, during the past two centuries, dozens of skeletons have been found in the canyon, along with bits and pieces of Spanish armor and mining gear. An abundance of Indian artifacts have also been found, suggesting a large Comanche encampment was once located near the mouth of the canyon.

Another legend is related to lost treasure. The Wichita Mountains are made up of rugged intrusive rock outcrops that originated millions of years ago as a result of deep and violent underground volcanic activity. The very forces that gave rise to these huge rock structures are the same ones associated with the formation of gold and silver, both of which are found in the range. During the early part of the seventeenth century, the Spanish invested a great deal of time exploring this region and attempted to establish a colony. While their colonization efforts failed, their mining activities succeeded, and legends describe the great wealth in gold and silver mined and shipped back to Mexico City headquarters or across the Atlantic Ocean to Spain.

Devil's Canyon was the site of a Spanish mission established in 1629 by Padre Juan de Salas. De Salas, along with a few Indian converts to Christianity, attempted to grow corn and beans near the mouth of the canyon where a small stream empties into the North Fork of the Red River. The tiny settlement languished for years, and then was abandoned in response to a prolonged drought.

More Spanish arrived at Devil's Canyon again in 1650. This time it was a small detachment of the army led by Captain Hernán Martín and adventurer Don Diego del Castillo. The party searched for gold and silver and, encouraged by discoveries of the ore, reported their findings to their superiors.

In 1657, a Spanish priest named Gilbert arrived at Devil's Canyon with a group of one hundred men. Employing directions provided by Martín and del Castillo, they located the gold deposits and began mining. A deep shaft – over one hundred feet – was sunk into the solid granite of the canyon floor. Several mule loads of ore were dug from the mine, but the area was abandoned because of the continued and growing threat of hostile Indians.

In 1698, a party of Spaniards disembarked at a port near New Orleans and undertook the long journey from the gulf coast to the Wichita Mountains. The expedition consisted of one hundred men equipped with mining tools along with a detachment of fifty soldiers. While the laborers and engineers dug the gold from the shaft, the soldiers were to keep the threat of raiding Indians to a minimum. Following a set of maps and charts, the Spaniards reached Devil's Canyon after a journey of several weeks. Once there, they established a permanent camp, constructed several dwellings of adobe and rock, and a church. In a nearby rock shelter they built a primitive smelter.

Time passed, and as the Spaniards mined and smelted the ore, the canyon was visited on occasion by Indians. At first, the visits were hostile, but when it became clear that the newcomers were only interested in the shiny colored rock they dug from the ground, a kind of truce was established and the Indians lost interest in them.

Several times each year, a mule train loaded with gold ingots would depart from Devil's Canyon and proceed to the port on the gulf. There, the gold was loaded onto a ship and transported across the ocean to Spain. The Spaniards would rest a few days in the growing city, purchase supplies and equipment, and make the long journey back to the Wichita Mountains.

As the months passed, the relations between the miners and the Indians grew tense. Though the Indians cared little for the Spaniards' activities in the canyon, they resented the impact the Europeans had on the game in the region. From time to time, soldiers would be sent out to hunt game to provide meat for the settlement. With each trip, they were forced to range farther afield because of the ongoing depletion of the herds of bison, deer, and antelope.

During some of these hunting expeditions, the soldiers were attacked by the Indians, and a few Spaniards were killed. When On entire hunting parties failed to return, it was presumed they were slaughtered by the Indians. The Spaniards found it necessary to post guards around the settlement day and night. By day, the Spaniards could see

Indians standing along the ridge tops observing them at their work.

Early one winter morning, a pack train consisting of fifty mules, each carrying a heavy load of gold, departed the canyon and headed southeastward toward the gulf. As the last mule passed through the mouth of the canyon, the Spaniards were attacked by what was later estimated to be more than two hundred mounted warriors. As the armed escort attempted to fight off the Indians, miners and soldiers from the settlement raced to the scene to assist their comrades. The result was inevitable, however, for within an hour all of the Spaniards lay dead save for three who escaped.

The area in and around Devil's Canyon remained quiet for several years. The only visitors were small hunting parties. In 1765, a French explorer named Brevel arrived in the area and made friends with the Indians who related the story of the slaughter of the Spaniards almost a century earlier. Brevel visited Devil's Canyon and noted the remains of the mining and smelting activity as well as the ruins of the old church and dwellings. He recorded his observations in his journal.

During the next several years, travelers and explorers to this region reported spotting the crumbling ruins of the Spanish structures and the remains of the mining activity. Despite the presence of gold, no one attempted to reopen the mines. During the 1830s, a party of Mexicans moved into the canyon and set up residence. A prevalent legend says that the Mexicans were led by a descendant of one of the survivors of the massacre that had occurred decades earlier. Carrying maps and descriptions of the great wealth to be found in Devil's Canyon, they located and reopened the mines.

In 1833, a man named Simon N. Cockrell, a scout for some businessmen who wanted to establish a trading post in the region, visited the canyon and observed the Mexicans hard at work in the mines. He reported that, though the Mexicans were friendly enough, they remained somewhat secretive relative to the mining activities.

During the summer of 1834, the Mexicans were preparing to leave Devil's Canyon with several dozen mule-loads of gold ore when they were set upon by a band of Kiowa Indians. A fierce battle erupted at the mouth of the canyon. Several of the Mexicans rushed to the gold mine and struggled to cover the entrance with large boulders. This done, they returned to the scene of the battle to aid their fellows. By the time they arrived, however, the fight was over and the Kiowa victorious. As the Indians went from body to body taking scalps, the surviving Mexicans concealed themselves among the boulders along one of the canyon walls and waited for the chance to escape.

Finished with scalping and mutilating the bodies, the Indians turned the pack train back into the canyon where they unloaded all of the ore, cached it in a cave in one canyon wall, and covered the entrance with several tons of rock and debris. Rounding up all of the now unburdened mules, the Indians left the canyon. When they thought it was safe, the Mexicans who were in hiding came forth and set out on foot for Mexico where months later they reported the massacre.

In 1850 a second group of Mexicans arrived at Devil's Canyon. Smaller than the earlier group, this one was led by one of the men who had escaped the attack by the Kiowa

Indians sixteen years earlier. On first entering the canyon, the Mexicans set up camp near a small pool of water just beyond the entrance. On the morning of the second day, they walked to the place where the Kiowa had cached the gold ore after the massacre. As the men labored to remove the rocks covering the cave, two young boys were sent to the trading post seven miles up the North Fork of the Red River to purchase some supplies. When the boys had traveled one-half mile after leaving the canyon, they heard gunfire and screams coming from where their comrades had been digging. Racing their horses back into the canyon, they spotted a large band of Indians attacking the party. The boys turned their mounts and rode for the trading post in hope of recruiting some help. Later, when they returned with a group of ten men, they discovered all of their companions had been killed and scalped.

The Wichita Mountains have also been claimed as home territory by numerous Indian tribes, including Comanche, Kiowa, and Wichita, all of which found the abundant game and water to their liking and perceived the rugged vastness as easy to defend against encroaching white settlers.

Anglo settlement and ranching in and around the Wichita Mountains began during the mid-nineteenth century. By 1880, several large and successful ranches had been established. The area came under the protection of the United States Army; several companies of well-mounted and well-armed cavalry were stationed in

During the early 1870s, a man named J. C. Settles established a large ranch near Devil's Canyon. From time to time while tending his cattle, Settles would ride into the canyon. There he spotted the remains of the old Spanish church and dwellings. Settles had heard tales of gold being mined from the canyon but did not believe them.

Settles made friends with many of the Indians who remained in the area and often hired some of them to work on his ranch. One afternoon Settles and an elderly Kiowa were running some cattle toward a pond in Devil's Canyon when the Indian related the story of the massacre of the Mexicans many years earlier. He also told Settles that he knew of a place back in the canyon where the Mexicans mined the ore and could take him to it. He told Settles that the miners had excavated a shaft over one hundred feet deep straight down into the solid rock of the canyon floor. He also explained how the Mexicans rolled large boulders over the opening to conceal it.

Though Settles was intrigued with this story, he was far too busy working his cattle ranch to take time off to investigate the old mine. Several years later, however, he invested some time and energy in a search. He located an ancient shaft that had been partially covered by a large boulder. With difficulty, he succeeded in blasting it from the opening. Inside the shaft, Settles found a human skeleton and what he described as a "coal-like substance" he couldn't identify. Without having any of the rock from the shaft assayed, Settles abandoned the mine, never to return.

In 1900, an aged Kiowa woman was seen hiking near Devil's Canyon. Those who saw her said it appeared as though she were searching for something. When questioned, the woman claimed that, as a young girl, she had accompanied the band of Kiowas that attacked and killed the Mexican miners in 1834. She said she had helped two warriors hide three mule loads of gold after the battle and she was now searching for them. Though the woman remained in the area for two weeks, she never found the cache.

In the years immediately after 1900, there was a spate of prospecting and mining activity in the Wichita Mountains. A number of entrepreneurs, geologists, engineers, and investors studied the prospects of Devil's Canyon. One prospector claimed to have found an eighty-five pound solid gold rock in one of the old Spanish mine shafts.

At the entrance to Devil's Canyon, there is a grove of trees, some of them very old. On several of these trees can be found the barely discernable evidence of ancient markings, among them an outline of what appears to be a turtle. The image of a turtle has long been recognized by researchers as a symbol used by the Spanish to denote the existence of gold or silver nearby.

Farther up the canyon is another turtle symbol, this one far more mysterious. It consists of a giant outline of a turtle on the ground, one that was constructed using a total of one hundred and fifty-two stones. The head of the turtle was pointing to a portion of the northwest wall of the canyon. Some have claimed that the turtle was oriented toward the location of one of the old Spanish mines. Unfortunately, this image was subsequently destroyed during the construction of a stock pond in the canyon.

One old Indian legend claims that the canyon is haunted by the devil himself and that he guards the cache of gold the Indians concealed in one cliff. The legend also says that a layer of human skeletons covers the gold. In 1967, a youth was hunting rabbits in Devil's Canyon when he discovered a newly exposed opening in one of the canyon walls. The area had been subjected to heavy rains the previous week and several hundred pounds of rock and debris had been washed away, exposing the cave beyond. Peering into the opening, the boy saw several skeletons. Believing he had come upon a long-forgotten burial chamber, the youth did not investigate any further. He told no one of his experience until several years later. On hearing the story, a group of men familiar with the tales and legends of the Spanish and Mexican gold mining activities in Devil's Canyon traveled to the location in attempt to locate the chamber and retrieve the gold. Though they spent several days searching for the old mines, they were unsuccessful.

Today, Devil's Canyon is part of Quartz Mountain State Park. The area is regularly visited by hikers and rock collectors. Some come to the canyon to search for evidence of the old Spanish and Mexican mines. If anyone has found the large cache of gold, they have not revealed it.

A Word About Sources

The decades invested in researching, studying, and searching looking for Oklahoma's lost mines and buried treasures have yielded hundreds of references: books, articles, newspaper accounts and interviews, local and regional historical journals, diaries, and more, most of which can be found on the Internet. In addition, dozens of interviews were conducted with people who had stories that had been passed down through the generations, people who had searched for the treasures and mines themselves, and had relatives who were involved in similar quests. One of the best resources is *Oklahoma Treasures and Treasure Tales* by Steve Wilson (University of Oklahoma Press, 1984). This well-researched book provided a starting point for many of my own adventures.

About the Author

W.C. Jameson is the award-winning author of seventy books, 1500 articles and essays, 300 songs, and dozens of poems. He is the best selling treasure author in the United States and his prominence as a professional fortune hunter had led to stints as a consultant for the *Unsolved Mysteries* television show and the Travel Channel. He served as an advisor for the film, *National Treasure* starring Nicolas Cage and appears in an interview on the DVD. His book, *Treasure Hunter: Caches, Curses, and Deadly Confrontations,* was named one of Indi Readers Best Books of the Year for 2011.

Jameson has written the sound tracks for two PBS documentaries and one feature film. His music has been heard on NPR and he wrote and performed in the musical, "Whatever Happened to the Outlaw, Jesse James?" Jameson has acted in five films and has been interviewed on The History Channel, The Travel Channel, PBS, and *Nightline*. When not working on a book, he tours the country as a speaker, conducting writing workshops and performing his music at folk festivals, concerts, roadhouses, and on television. He lives in Llano, Texas.